THE INTERIM

THE INTERIM

A GUIDE TO TRANSITION LEADERSHIP IN HIGHER EDUCATION

DANIEL J. BERNARDO

WSU PRESS

Washington State University Press
Pullman, Washington

Washington State University Press
PO Box 645910
Pullman, Washington 99164-5910
Phone: 800-354-7360
Email: wsupress@wsu.edu
Website: wsupress.wsu.edu

Library of Congress Cataloging-in-Publication Data

Names: Bernardo, Daniel J., 1958- author.
Title: The interim : a guide to transition leadership in higher education /
   by Daniel J. Bernardo.
Description: Pullman, Washington : Washington State University Press,
   [2022] | Includes bibliographical references and index.
Identifiers: LCCN 2022007617 | ISBN 9780874224139 (Paperback)
Subjects: LCSH: Education, Higher--Administration. | Interim executives.
Classification: LCC LB2341 .B4764 2022 | DDC 378.1/01--dc23/eng/20220425
LC record available at https://lccn.loc.gov/2022007617

The Washington State University Pullman campus is located on the homelands of the Niimíipuu (Nez Perce) Tribe and the Palus people. We acknowledge their presence here since time immemorial and recognize their continuing connection to the land, to the water, and to their ancestors. WSU Press is committed to publishing works that foster a deeper understanding of the Pacific Northwest and the contributions of its Native peoples.

Cover design by Jeffry E. Hipp

Dedication

Dedicated to my wife, Pamela, who provided unwavering support throughout my twenty-five-year administrative career, and the many mentors and colleagues I depended upon along the way.

• • •

Contents

List of Illustrations

List of Tables

Introduction

The summer of 2015, when I stepped in as interim president of Washington State University (WSU), the school was going through a tumultuous time; our revered and charismatic president of eight years, Dr. Elson S. Floyd, had suddenly passed away. The news rocked the university—most people did not know that he was terminally ill. The president had just gained legislative approval for WSU to start the state's second medical school—the university's most ambitious initiative in thirty years—and we were preparing its launch.

During my second week in the role, I arrived at work one morning to find three members of the FBI in my office. They advised me that an unnamed Eastern European country had gained access to our campus network and was using the platform to spearfish federal agencies such as the US Departments of Defense and Energy. They warned that ill-planned attempts to extract them from the network could result in the perpetrators crashing the system, incapacitating our entire IT network just prior to the start of the academic year. Two weeks later, intense forest fires around the Pacific Northwest created an air quality problem that posed a public health threat to vulnerable people and shut down airline service to the campus. Air quality worsened and threatened the beginning of the fall semester.

As the semester approached, campus phones and email accounts were bombarded one Monday morning with calls and messages from citizens complaining about the contents of some syllabi posted online for three "Comparative Ethnic Studies" classes. A conservative watchdog group had found the syllabi on the Web and contacted FOX News, which aired the story over the weekend, (correctly) alleging that statements in the syllabi infringed on students' free speech.

Looking forward to something positive, I noted that the next Saturday was the beginning of football season. What could be better than a WSU home game to boost the spirits of faculty, staff, students, and alumni?

Unfortunately, the Cougars suffered their most humiliating defeat in years, losing to a team that played one division below us.

A month later, however, all was well. After four weeks of preparation, the intruders were successfully extracted from the network. The smoke cleared enough for the semester to begin, and actions were taken to assure the safety of faculty, staff, and students. Meetings with the faculty who authored the syllabi, while tense, resulted in their making the necessary modifications to assure students' First Amendment rights were not violated. The Cougars won their next four games.

This story is illustrative of the trials and tribulations of interim executive leaders in higher education. My initial reaction was, of course, "What have I gotten myself into? Is this a typical month in the life of a university president?" Interim leaders are thrust into positions for which they likely have little direct experience, often with little preparation, and sometimes at the most inopportune times. But by drawing upon their past experiences, accessing their already developed leadership skills, and securing the support of people around them, they can have a positive experience and provide critical service to their institutions.

This book serves as a handbook for people who have assumed or are considering taking on interim leadership positions in higher education. It provides a step-by-step guide to assist interim leaders in navigating the period before, during, and after their interim service and helps them derive the most benefit from the experience

WHY IS INTERIM LEADERSHIP IMPORTANT?

Transitions are inevitable in every organization. Institutions are dynamic, not static; and one component of organizational change is leadership turnover (Zaniello 2019). Even so, the turnover in executive positions in higher education has escalated in recent years and is becoming increasingly problematic. Interim leadership can contribute to institutional instability and a lack of momentum in driving progress toward university goals.

The 2018 Administrators in Higher Education Survey (Bichsel et al. 2018), conducted by the College and University Professional Association for Human Resources (CUPA-HR), revealed that the median tenure of university presidents was five years while the median time in position for provosts and deans was approximately three to four years. Recent data reported by Higher Ed Direct (2018) indicates that presidents/chancellors, provosts, and deans experience the highest turnover of any positions in higher education. Of the 3,893 provosts listed in the 2017 *Higher Education Directory*, 808—or 21 percent—were new the following year. Turnover rates for presidents and chancellors ranked second at 18 percent, followed by deans at 16 to 22 percent, depending upon the discipline.

While the reasons for this accelerated turnover are not well understood, it is clear from the management literature that low job satisfaction is a leading contributor. Certainly, mounting political, financial, and administrative pressures are driving qualified people from these positions. Such pressures can also contribute to leaders being unsuccessful in their roles, resulting in involuntary turnover.

Some argue that a lack of prepared administrative talent is also contributing to turnover. Many universities have traditionally hired from within to minimize risk, but fewer people are interested in these positions. According to the American Council on Higher Education, 60 percent of presidents at doctoral-granting universities served as provosts prior to accepting their presidency; however, a recent survey of provosts found that only 30 percent planned to pursue a presidency.

Accelerated turnover and the need for interim leaders also points to systemic problems within the academy concerning leadership development. Most institutions do not engage in formal succession planning to identify and prepare future leaders. With the exception of a handful of programs sponsored by professional associations, few formal leadership development opportunities are available (Gmelch and Buller 2015). At WSU, we established the Provost's Leadership Academy to develop the leadership skills of a cohort of thirty to thirty-five faculty each year. That program was highly successful in identifying and preparing future leaders. Some similar programs exist across the academy, but they are not the norm. Similarly, some colleges and universities have instituted formal succession planning for their dean and department chair positions, but again, that is the exception and not the rule. Until more dramatic steps are taken, most institutions will continue to place good people who are ill-prepared to step into interim roles, using a "trial by fire" approach.

Contrast this situation with the private sector, where greater emphasis is placed on leadership succession planning and building the skill set of next-generation leaders. Most corporations know the cost of executive leadership turnover; when a departure occurs, they are prepared to move a successor into the position. If they do elect to conduct an external search, it is done in an expeditious manner with the expectation that the new leader will be in place within months. The not-for-profit sector has developed a cadre of experienced individuals who will take on interim leadership roles through training programs offered by organizations such as the Third Sector Company. But again, these "administrators for hire" are not prevalent in higher education.

The combination of accelerated turnover and longer periods of service in interim roles is translating to leadership crises at some institutions, where a quarter or more of executive positions may be filled by interim leaders at any one time. A common attribute of most institutions that have achieved significant progress in recent years is continuity of executive leadership. Similarly, if one studies colleges within a university, it is typically the ones with stable and effective leadership within the dean's office that are excelling. Like sports teams that are always changing coaches, academic organizations that are constantly being whipsawed by leadership changes have significant challenges in maintaining forward momentum.

The pervasiveness of interim leaders throughout the academy makes it imperative that we focus on better defining the role of interim leaders and improving their performance. No longer can stretches of interim leadership be viewed as transitory periods where nothing gets done. If the interim's role is simply that of a placeholder, the institution will likely miss opportunities and suffer long-term consequences. The first order of business is to better prepare interim leaders for the task at hand and empower them to lead.

The following discussion from the *Chronicle of Higher Education*'s online forum vividly illustrates the point.

> **Question:** Has anyone dealt with a changing administration? I'm a relatively new faculty member who has become involved in university-wide governance. We have a newly appointed interim provost who is less than inspiring, and we are becoming anxious about our budget, the future of our programs....

Answer: I've dealt with several interim administrators. Most are fairly benign because they really don't have much power. Occasionally, you'll find some nut in an interim job and the power will go to his head. Unless the president has advised the interim to make some dramatic changes, my guess is that nothing much will happen. The interim, if applying for the permanent job, will not want to tick anyone off. If not applying, there's really no point in making dramatic decisions that might be undone when the permanent provost arrives.

The respondent demonstrates a very narrow and suspicious view of interim leadership and an expectation that the interim will simply maintain the status quo. This perspective is common among university faculty and staff and is reflective of a culture of complacency about interim leadership that pervades many institutions.

There is a universal lack of understanding about interim leadership. Despite all the books and articles published on executive leadership, there is a dearth of writing on interim leadership, either in general or specific to higher education. This was a surprising finding, given the recent proliferation of interim positions and the fact that there is no shortage of books written about administration and leadership within the academy.

When I contacted a colleague who is very familiar with the scholarship in higher education administration about this idea, he confirmed that he was not aware of any books on the topic and noted that some universities have used Robbins and Finley's *The Accidental Leader: What to Do When You're Suddenly in Charge* (2003). There are a couple of challenges with this book as applied to higher education. First, it is written from a business and industry perspective and focuses on leaders at the manager level as opposed to executive leaders. As such, it really does not transfer well to higher education. Second, there is nothing accidental about interim leadership in higher education. Interim leadership needs to be taken on in a thoughtful, strategic, and planful manner.

As someone who has served in three different interim executive roles at major public institutions, I developed an understanding of many of the unique challenges of interim leadership the same way that many higher education leaders learned their craft—trial by fire. After the third iteration, I thought about the need to document some of the lessons learned so that others might have a better starting point going into their interim leadership position.

KEY DIFFERENCES BETWEEN INTERIM AND PERMANENT LEADERSHIP

There are several important differences between interim and permanent leadership ("How is Interim Leadership Different" 2017). While most of the skills required of any leader within higher education also apply to interim leaders, the scope and circumstances of the interim role create some unique challenges.

First, the circumstances under which many interim leaders enter their position can create a unique and complex administrative environment unlike that which someone filling the position permanently will encounter. Paramount to this challenging environment is an absence of preparation time prior to assuming the administrative role. Unlike permanent leaders who contemplate whether they should apply for a position, prepare for interviews, and have the benefit of what is often a lengthy period between accepting the position and actually stepping into the role, interims are often thrust into it with little warning or preparation. The ability to step in and quickly assess a situation, build productive relationships with the team, and plan and execute short-term goals are all critical skills for an interim leader.

A second and related distinction is that interim leaders have a more short-term scope of issues. The most pressing demands on their time are keeping the day-to-day activities of the unit moving forward. It is likely that there are several projects or issues their predecessor was dealing with that require immediate attention. Issues identified that need to be addressed prior to hiring a permanent successor also require immediate attention. Even though interims' period of service may be longer than that of their private sector counterparts, it still represents a compressed time span within which to execute necessary organizational change.

Third, interim leaders focus on preparing for their successors. Setting up their successor for success is almost always a goal communicated by the person or board appointing the interim to the position. Oftentimes, addressing this need involves tackling issues or activities that limited the success of the predecessor. Thus, interim leadership requires a selfless leadership style and recognition that the reins will soon be turned over to the permanent successor ("The Unconventional Value of an Interim Leader").

Relative to permanent leaders, interim leaders can feel less empowered to lead and face unexpected responses from individuals within and outside the organization. Despite the need to change the culture of complacency referenced above, this behavior prevails in most higher education institutions. The ability to recognize and address this culture is critical to success in an interim role. Moving the organization forward and breaking down impediments to change are important roles of the interim leader.

On the other hand, there are some advantages that interim leaders possess relative to their permanent successors. Most importantly, impermanence can have value. Temporary status and perceived neutrality can be used to open lines of communication and implement change without fear of sacrificing long-term relationships. Interim leaders have the unique opportunity to make changes without enduring the long-term personal consequences that a permanent leader might need to consider. The old saying, "No good crisis should go to waste," might apply here. While appointment of an interim leader should not create a crisis, it does present a unique opportunity to implement needed change.

FOCUS AND ORGANIZATION OF THIS BOOK

Because this book's principal audience is people taking on interim roles, it is written in a concise style to provide maximum information in a short read. The material focuses on executive leadership positions in higher education—deans, vice presidents, provosts, and presidents—but most of the information is applicable to other roles, both within and outside higher education.

One finding from research conducted for this book was that successful interim leadership is significantly influenced by those who appoint and supervise interim leaders as well as the employees who support them. Thus, the information provided is useful not only for people filling interim roles but also for executives who manage them and personnel who support interim leaders.

Much of the information provided has been developed from interviews with people who have served as interim deans, vice presidents, provosts, and presidents.[1] Over thirty former and current interim leaders were interviewed, and several of their stories have been distributed throughout this text to illustrate real-life examples of some of the points being

1. For the sake of brevity, the term "president" is synonymous with "chancellor" or any other title for the chief executive officer of a college or university.

made. These individuals provided excellent input into the challenges they encountered and how the interim experience can be improved. To protect the anonymity of these individuals, pseudonyms were used to identify the people in the case studies. Individuals in key positions who interact with interim leaders—e.g., executive assistants, finance officers, development directors—were also interviewed to gain their insights, as were executives who supervised interim leaders.

An important observation from these interviews is that those who have successfully served in interim executive positions come from a mixture of backgrounds and employ a variety of different leadership styles. There are many leadership styles—servant leader, democratic, transactional, laissez-faire, coaching, situational, and benevolent dictator, to name a few. The leadership style of most leaders is likely best characterized as a hybrid of two or more of these. This book does not advocate for any one in particular, as most of the findings and recommendations can be applied with any leadership style. The only suggestion I have on this topic is to be yourself and employ the style that you are most comfortable with and that fits the situation.

This book is oriented toward helping interim leaders have the greatest possible impact during their tenure in the role. Not one of the interim leaders interviewed was directed by a superior to maintain the status quo or serve as a placeholder until the replacement arrived. The recommendations made in this book are focused on assisting the interim leader and the organization in their efforts to achieve sustained and meaningful outcomes during the interim period. As a president of a prestigious public university said when interviewed for this book, "Regardless of whether we have the tag 'interim' or not, we are all interims, it's just [a matter of] how long the interim period is."

For individuals with some administrative experience, much of the information in this book is not new, but it can serve as a good reminder and place past experiences in a more useful context. Also, if you pull out just a few useful nuggets to apply in your own professional life, this book will have been a worthwhile read.

The interim leadership assignment is divided into five distinct stages (see Figure I.1). The first is positioning yourself for success. In chapter 1 we investigate the circumstances by which leaders take on interim positions and the various roles they may be asked to perform. The second stage focuses on leveraging the front end—the time period between accepting the position and the first day on the job. Stage three corresponds to the first thirty days on the job. Chapters 2 and 3 provide insights into how to effectively execute the transition into an interim position—planning for the new role, developing your thirty-day plan, and executing the first thirty days. The fourth stage involves evolving leadership, practices, and culture during the remainder of the interim period. Chapters 4 through 8 address key administrative functions that executive leaders in higher education encounter—things like time management, working with a new team, change management, fiscal management, and external relations—but placed in the context of interim leadership. Chapter 9 focuses on building a functional support network and taking care of yourself while serving in a leadership position. The fifth stage concentrates on executing the handoff—the time period between the announcement of a new permanent leader's appointment and the actual arrival date—and is the focus of chapter 10.

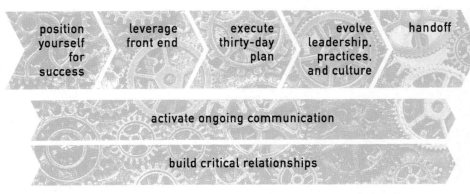

Figure I.1. Interim Leadership Timeline: Five Stages of Interim Leadership

Chapter 1

"TO INTERIM OR NOT TO INTERIM," THAT IS THE QUESTION

The provost announces that he is leaving the university to take on a presidency at another university. You have been approached by the president about stepping away from your current dean position and taking on the interim provost role. Can you be successful in this interim role? Is this a positive step for you personally? Does it fit into your professional aspirations? These are all-important questions that must be considered as you evaluate the leadership opportunity at hand.

IS THIS THE RIGHT OPPORTUNITY FOR YOU?

Research for this book made clear that there are numerous circumstances under which people take on interim leadership roles. They are usually asked because they are regarded as "good citizens" in the organization and trusted colleagues. The opportunity to hold a major leadership role can appear validating and intellectually invigorating. You might imagine you can fix many things that appear to be broken.

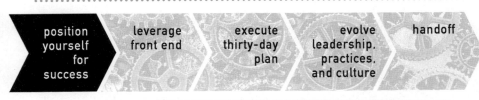

Figure 1.1. Interim Leadership Timeline, Stage 1: Position Yourself for Success

Regardless of the situation or your intentions, you must go into the position with eyes wide open. For some, this decision can become the proverbial fork in the road in which their career trajectory is supported and enhanced or, conversely, delayed or derailed. Thus, the decision to interim or not is a serious one. It can be a remarkable leadership development opportunity and allow you to explore in real time the complexities, opportunities, and challenges of executive leadership; or it can be a poor experience with a low probability of success for even the most seasoned leader (Vaillancourt 2018).

As with most administrative decisions, determining whether to accept an interim post involves weighing the personal and professional benefits against the risks. Several benefits have already been discussed. They include experience, professional development, increased compensation, visibility, and the self-actualization associated with helping the institution. Bradt, Check, and Lawler (2016) define three sources of risk when someone takes on a new leadership role: personal risk, role risk, and organizational risk:

- **Personal risk** is defined by how well the role fits your strengths and ambitions. Obviously, the greater the difference between your own background and the skills required for the position, the lower the probability of success and the higher the personal risk. Similarly, if the position does not provide an experience relevant to the direction you want your career to take, there is a greater probability that the position will not be a fulfilling experience.

- **Role risk** relates to the roles and responsibilities of the position and their clarity. As we will investigate further in chapter 9, role ambiguity is the largest source of uncertainty among interim leaders. The greater your uncertainty and the lack of clarity about the position's roles and responsibilities, the greater the role risk.

- **Organizational risk** is derived from the culture and competency of the organization for which you are considering taking on a leadership role. Let's face it; not all organizations possess a positive culture or are particularly competent in meeting their institutional mission. These organizations are difficult to lead; the greater the dysfunction, the greater the organizational risk you are exposing yourself to.

Assessing the Opportunity

It is critical to do your due diligence before accepting a position. Due diligence is the exercise of collecting information from multiple sources to analyze the opportunities and risks of a position. There are many colleagues who may have useful perspectives. Most obvious is the person departing from the position. For whatever reasons, this person is often an underutilized resource by interim leaders. There are some unique circumstances where this person might not be a good resource—e.g., the predecessor is terminated—but for most situations, the successor is more than willing to discuss the challenges and opportunities of the role.

Individuals within the unit can also be excellent sources of information. If you are filling the role from within the university, a trusted colleague within the administrative unit can provide an unvarnished look inside. Individuals in similar positions within or outside the institution may also provide useful insights. One fact that experienced academic leaders eventually discover is that their experiences are not all that unique to their institution. For example, deans serving at similar colleges or universities have very similar challenges, opportunities, and frustrations, so talking to a dean colleague at another institution can provide valuable insights to someone considering an interim dean position. Similarly, talking to a dean within the institution can yield some excellent intelligence into whether an interim position is the right role for you.

Without exception, interim leaders interviewed cited the importance of organizational culture to their success (or lack of it) in the position. Bradt, Check, and Lawler (2016) use the BRAVE acronym in defining the five components of organizational culture—behaviors, relationships, attitudes, values, and environment. The BRAVE framework (Figure 1.2) is easy to apply and provides a structured way to identify, think about, and talk about culture:

- **Behaviors** are about how the organization acts in carrying out its functions. Do members work more as a team or as independent actors? Is behavior fluid and flexible or highly structured? Do members tend to seek out partnerships with other entities or limit the scope of their problem-solving activities to within the organization?

- **Relationships** reflect how the organization connects. Do people communicate formally or informally? Is decision-making diffused or more autocratic? Do people identify more with the organization as a whole or as subgroup members?

- **Attitudes** have to do with how the organization approaches its mission. Are people more proactive or reactive? Is there a bias toward innovation and creating new ideas or acting in response to others' needs and demands? Do people tend to respond to challenges and opportunities with a resource-constrained or opportunity-seeking mindset?

- **Values** are about what matters to the organization, its members, and why. What is the organization's mission (why), vision (what), and values (how)? Are these interpreted as more intended and evolving or more written and set? Are these values shared across the organization, and do they drive behavior?

- **Environment** defines the playing field for the organization. Is the focus more on opportunities to capture or problems to solve? Are the progress and growth drivers more human, societal, technical, or interpersonal? Are the organization's main barriers external hurdles or internal capabilities?

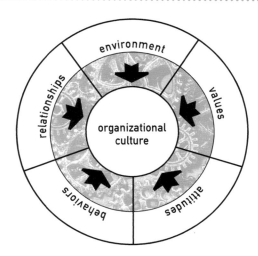

Figure 1.2. BRAVE Culture Assessment Model

A BRAVE culture assessment involves doing some research on each of these elements and thinking about how well the composite culture fits you and your leadership style. Some leaders are more adept at leading organizations with specific cultural characteristics. While interim leaders can certainly help shape culture, it is unlikely that they will be able to radically change it. It is therefore important to be realistic about whether you can manage within the broad cultural context that you inherit.

Questions to Ask Yourself

The decision to take on an interim leadership role requires serious self-reflection. Some useful questions to ask yourself as you contemplate an interim leadership opportunity follow (Pichon 2018):

- **Is this position a good match for my skills and background?**
  Given your due diligence, can you be successful and is the organization's culture a good match? What is the level of personal risk associated with the position?

- **Is the level of support for the position sufficient to achieve success?**
  The required level of support can take on many forms. First, is there a competent and inspired leadership team surrounding the position? Is there adequate administrative support? Also, will you have support from the next level administrator who is hiring you?

- **Why is this position open?**
  The best situations are typically those that arise when the incumbent leaves the position for reasons of promotion or retirement. For example, an interim provost is needed because the provost went on to become a university president. Remember, there are sometimes important reasons why an incumbent leaves a position. An open executive position with a history of turnover is likely a signal of long-term structural or cultural problems. There are positions in which even the most seasoned leaders will encounter difficulties being successful. Avoid these positions at all costs.

- **What's in it for me?**
  This is a perfectly appropriate question. While service to the organization is a laudable goal, you should also benefit personally in the form of

professional development and personal gain. In many ways, an interim position is an opportunity to earn more money, demonstrate the skills required for the permanent position, or enhance your professional reputation. By virtue of being in this position, you are likely to gain new connections, greater visibility, and deeper administrative experience and be able to advance new ideas (Vaillancourt 2018). As the availability of potential candidates for executive positions continues to decline, executive search firms are increasingly looking to those who have served or are serving in interim roles. That being the case, serving in an interim role may well open up professional opportunities in the future.

Depending upon the circumstances, interim service can be an excellent professional development opportunity. It is important to consciously frame the position to maximize professional development outcomes.

Most interim leaders interviewed felt fairly compensated for their services. While interim leaders need not be compensated at a level equal to an experienced predecessor, they should receive a salary commensurate with their experience and responsibilities.

- **Will I enjoy the job?**
Job satisfaction is important, even in the short run. Taking on new challenges can be invigorating to some, but for people who enjoy calm and comfort in their position, an interim role might not be the best fit.

- **How will it feel to go back to my previous role?**
From the interviews conducted, it is clear this question deserves serious attention. In the event you accept the interim position and later return to your previous post (voluntarily or not), you will need to understand the transition process (when and how this will occur).

Whether real or perceived, there can be an aura of power and control associated with the interim position. You need to ask yourself, "Can I live with having to return to the lower ranks once the assignment ends?" For many, this is very uncomfortable because, instead of leading, you are now following again. This change may upset your routine and make you feel marginalized or undervalued (Vaillancourt 2018). As one former interim dean who returned to his former position noted, "Your relationships will never be the same." On the positive side, you will likely experience new and deeper relationships with executive leaders, external stakeholders, and so forth. Conversely, peers can hold grudges based on decisions made during your time as interim leader. Interestingly, several former interim deans noted that serving in the role seemed to invoke negative reactions toward them on the part of the successor.

- **How will serving in this role impact my scholarly endeavors?**
  This is a particularly important question for interim deans. Several past interim deans noted that serving in the role created a challenge of reinvigorating their research program and regaining previous momentum.

Questions to Ask the Person Offering You the Position

An important part of your due diligence is to have a thorough conversation with the person offering you the interim role. This meeting is a chance for you to gain clarity on the position and the terms under which you would be operating should you elect to accept it. The nature of this conversation will depend on the situation, but here are a few questions you might want to consider:

- **What are the responsibilities and parameters of the position?**
  It is critical to gain clarity on the position's roles and responsibilities. Are you responsible for all aspects of the position as defined by the predecessor's role or an amended version of the position? This includes being clear about the reporting lines—who you will report to and who will report to you. Knowing your supervisor's expectations will help you determine whether this is a good next step for you.

- **What are the primary outcomes you wish to achieve during the period of interim leadership?**
  A competent executive should have some very explicit outcomes for you to achieve during the interim leader's tenure. It is important to have a clear understanding of these deliverables prior to accepting the position. If the executive does not have any specific outcomes, that could be a red flag.

- **What is the process being used to fill the interim appointment?**
  Interim roles can be filled through a number of processes—internal searches, external searches, direct appointment, or use of an external

employment firm, to name a few. Formal competitive processes tend to provide legitimacy, and in some cases can enhance the probability of success. Assuring that the approach being used fits the situation is a worthwhile conversation to have with the person offering the position.

- **Can I be considered as a candidate for the permanent role if I decide I am interested?**
  Some universities make it a practice to exclude interims from consideration. Personally, I don't see the wisdom in such a policy. Sometimes people accept an interim role for which they have no long-term interest, only to find out they actually enjoy the work. Therefore, it is useful to have that option available.

Gain as much clarification as possible on roles, responsibilities, and expectations from the person(s) appointing you to the interim position. Such clarity will minimize the probability of a disagreement during the appointment or after it is completed.

As an interim president, Thomas was approached by the board chair one month into the interim appointment, requesting that he not apply for the permanent position. The governing board had just met to discuss the search for a new president and decided that they wanted to recruit a president from outside the university. The board chair explained that this decision had nothing to do with Thomas's performance to date, but the board believed his strong leadership and interim experience would likely scare off capable applicants. The chair requested that the interim president make a public announcement that he would not be seeking the permanent position, which would then allow for the recruitment of a stronger applicant pool. Thomas really had no choice other than to comply, as it was clear that the governing board was interested in an external candidate and would not select him if he chose to apply.

This situation was poorly handled by the board, which should have put this condition up front when asking the interim to serve. Thomas wished that he had clarified the issue prior to accepting the position. While he would likely have chosen not to apply, the directive adversely affected the relationship between him and the board.

- **How long will the appointment last?**
  There should be an explicit time frame attached to the appointment. If there is not, insist upon it or at least upon a time when you and the supervisor will reevaluate continuation.

  Ordinarily, interim assignments last between six and eighteen months (Shellenbarger 2016). Be aware that universities are filled with "interim" leaders whose appointments have been extended several times beyond the original agreed-upon time period. Vaillancourt (2018) recommends establishing a check-in date for you to determine the progress of a final decision being made as to whether your role will be transformed into a permanent position assignment or a job search will be initiated for a permanent replacement.

  About half of the interim leaders surveyed indicated that they were provided with a specific term for the appointment (normally one year). Of those provided with a specified term, only about half found that the time period was adhered to.

- **Will I be expected to do this job in addition to my regular role?**
  Taking an interim position while being expected to serve in your regular position can be a sure way to fail at both. Do not fall into this trap. It is critical to gain a full or significant reprieve from the responsibilities of your past position. This issue is discussed in further detail in chapter 2.

FRAMING THE POSITION FOR PERSONAL AND ORGANIZATIONAL SUCCESS

As when contemplating any potential new job, it is important to position yourself for success, both personally and in terms of the organization you will be leading. Important components of success include assuring that you have: (1) sufficient time to allocate to the new role, (2) the resource base needed to get the job done, and (3) a definition of the role that maximizes your own professional development.

As noted above, trying to manage an interim role in addition to your previous position is a recipe for burnout and ineffectiveness. It is critical that you shed as many of your current responsibilities as possible. For interim deans, for example, this means leaving behind as many teaching, research, and advising responsibilities as is practically possible and developing a coverage plan to assure that these responsibilities are met. For administrators taking on a position up the administrative ladder, this means identifying a member of your team who can step into your former role. Such a move will provide a great professional development opportunity for a capable subordinate.

It is extremely difficult for some people to leave past responsibilities behind. They often find themselves looking over the shoulder of the person filling their former role. While this may be understandable, given that interim leaders have a significant personal investment in their former unit and may be returning to their former position, this behavior should be avoided. Such oversight can be stifling to both the former unit and its new leader and divert your time and attention away from the task at hand. If you are not comfortable with the coverage plan, you should probably decline the interim leadership opportunity.

Rarely in higher education administration do we feel adequately resourced, but you do want to make certain that you have enough resources to get the job done. Of course, as the unit's executive leader, you do control resource allocation, but you need to be careful not to have an appearance of moving an inordinate share of resources to advance your own role.

A couple of interim leaders surveyed were proud that they were able to gain financial commitments from their college president or provost in exchange for their services. It may be appropriate in the short run to help fill holes created by your departure, but extorting long-term commitments for your service in an interim role is not behavior one would expect from a true leader.

Finally, think ahead about the professional development outcomes you want from the experience. If you aren't conscious of these outcomes, the day-to-day activities will consume you and the opportunity will pass. It can be useful to make a list of skills and knowledge areas in which you are seeking to gain more experience. Factoring in these considerations prior to stepping into the position allows you and your supervisor to agree up front on this dimension of the job.

INTERIM LEADERSHIP SCENARIOS

Interim leadership positions can take a variety of forms and evolve from a variety of circumstances. These circumstances create unique roles for the interim leader that require specific approaches to the position.

Circumstances Creating the Need for Interim Leadership

The need for interim leadership can arise from various circumstances, planned or unplanned:

- **Resignation/Retirement**
  The majority of interim leadership opportunities fall into this category. These opportunities can be the least difficult, as there tends to be more time to plan a transition and fewer "land mines" to navigate.

- **Death**
  Following someone who has died while in office can be very challenging, as the shock and sadness associated with the incumbent's death places additional responsibilities on the interim leader. People respond differently to these situations—sadness, anger, blame, and so on—and you need to be prepared for all types of reactions.

- **Termination**
  Unfortunately, these situations are becoming increasingly common. Included in this category are situations that might be publicly communicated as a resignation, but the resignation was negotiated as an alternative to termination. There are many possible scenarios that could have precipitated this situation; three that were found to be most common were the incumbent's ineffectiveness in the position; an inability to get along with the supervisor; or a behavioral issue, event, or indiscretion that required the incumbent to immediately vacate the position.

- **Leave of Absence**
  Situations where the interim leader is preceded and succeeded by the same executive make up this category. There are many circumstances that might require an interim leader to step in for the permanent leader. Among the most common are maternity leave, short- or long-term disability, sabbatical, and personal leave.

Roles of the Interim Leader

Each of these initial circumstances requires unique responses and strategies from the interim leader. On the whole, the role of the interim leader is dependent upon several factors, including the reason for the predecessor's absence, the health of the organization, and the need for organizational change. Five broad roles of interim leaders follow:

Executive Transition Interim

The executive transition interim provides organizational leadership following the vacating of an executive position. In most cases the successor is unknown, and the interim is afforded opportunities to lead advancement in all facets of the organization—e.g., programmatic, fiscal, and personnel. In these cases, the interim leader is typically working within the boundaries of the inherited organizational structure, mission, and program portfolio.

The case of an interim leadership opportunity resulting from the death of the incumbent deserves special mention. Pacing is critical in these situations. Pushing forward aggressively is not a recommended strategy, as people will need time to grieve and adjust to the sudden departure of their leader. This situation is one where patience will get you to the desired end more quickly than aggressive leadership. Celebrating the successes and legacy of the deceased leader is not only the right thing to do, but it will define you as an understanding and caring leader to members of the team.

Patience and timing are critical determinants of success in an interim role. Different situations will require alternative strategies in how quickly you can move forward with key initiatives.

Claire, a former interim dean, had the misfortune to follow a longtime beloved dean who suddenly passed away in office. Tragically, the interim dean who initially replaced the longtime dean died suddenly after two weeks on the job. An important quality of interim leaders is courage, and it was truly a courageous act to follow these two tragic losses. Fortunately, the old tale that bad things happen in threes did not pan out. Claire worked tirelessly to assist the college through this difficult time.

Before engaging in any discussions about moving forward, she made certain that colleagues had a number of opportunities to grieve and express their feelings in a variety of different ways. She took advantage of several occasions, both within and outside the college, to celebrate the achievements of the deceased dean. Although the college needed a significant refresh following the tenure of the longtime dean, Claire did not rush to initiate these discussions, waiting several months before beginning this work. Starting with her leadership team, she began to sensitize them to the topic, gained the support of the leadership team, and then gradually rolled out ideas to the faculty and staff. Frequent and transparent communication proved to be the most important strategy for navigating this difficult situation.

"Clean Up the Mess" Interim

Unfortunately, interim leaders sometimes replace unsuccessful executives and are charged with cleaning up the mess that was left behind. Interim leaders who inherited these situations cited significant personnel, programmatic, financial, and/or morale issues that required immediate attention. The absolute priority of the interim leader in these cases is to reinstill confidence in the organization and its leadership. Skilled interim leadership can transform this time of turmoil and transition into an opportunity for the organization to redefine itself. The interim can use the postmortem period to gain critical insights into the situation that created failure and begin the process of building a functional organization.

Sometimes the lack of success of the predecessor can be traced back to personnel issues that were unaddressed and contributed to low morale and a poor workplace environment. In these cases, the most important role of the interim is to come in and assess the situation, identify the root cause, and correct the problem.

A former interim dean, Samantha inherited a college with a history of bullying, sexual harassment, and discrimination. Unfortunately, through inaction of previous leadership, a culture of tolerance of this behavior was present. A couple of the offenders were highly successful faculty who felt insulated from discipline in response to their transgressions. Samantha quickly took on a couple of high-profile cases that ultimately resulted in disciplinary action against several faculty. She invited the university's human resources unit to assess the workplace environment. In addition, she initiated an educational program to make certain that everyone in the college was aware of university policies concerning the work environment and discrimination and that they were able to identify and feel safe reporting bad behavior. Several department chairs were aware of these past situations but felt that they lacked support from the dean's office to take them on. Others just chose to ignore them. Samantha put all unit leaders on notice that they were to report any and all allegations. While personnel actions remained private, word quickly got around that things had changed, thus initiating the first steps of cultural change.

Samantha had done a great service for her permanent replacement, who was able to continue to advance this issue as a key initiative during his first year in office. Sometimes moving these situations through the necessary administrative steps takes time and focus that can get lost in leadership transitions, but the new dean made certain that did not happen. The work to initiate investigations and document past events was instrumental in removing a couple of bad actors from the college.

"Leave of Absence" Interim

This interim provides a temporary solution for a defined length of time, stepping in for a professional who plans to return to the position (Wilcox 2018). This is almost always a maintenance role, and the situation can be challenging in that the expectation of the incumbent's return can limit the power and authority of the interim. Nonetheless, the organization must continue to move forward during this interim period.

To the extent possible, it is important to communicate to the team the length of the interim leadership period and the direction provided by the permanent leader. Typically, leave of absence interims are operating within the inherited structure, policies, and procedures of the organization. Executive leadership often takes on more of a mentoring role in this setting as team members are knowledgeable of their own roles and how individuals interact as a team.

New Executive Position Interim

Sometimes the creation of a new unit will be accompanied by the appointment of an interim leader. The new unit might be the result of organizational restructuring; for example, dividing into two units—budget/finance and administrative services—the massive area led by a vice president for finance and administration. Similarly, academic restructuring might result in the creation of a new college that combines units, people, and resources from multiple academic areas.

This situation places the interim in the unique position where transitioning the unit or organization to a permanent leader takes on the greatest importance. These can be complex situations characterized by high anxiety and great excitement, and the success of this early period of a unit's formation can go a long way in defining its long-term trajectory. Typically, the interim leader is charged with developing an organizational structure, establishing policies and procedures, forming committees, and so on. The interim leader must develop sufficient structure to make the new unit functional while leaving enough flexibility for the inaugural permanent leader to build the new organization.

Although these structural elements can present their own challenges, the most daunting task may be initiating the process of defining the culture of the new unit. Oftentimes, culture is something that is difficult to pin down; as a result, leaders may steer away from addressing culture. However, it's very important to work with members of the team to clearly define the culture you are trying to build.

If the new organization has been created from the merger of two or more units, the challenge is even more complex, as merging cultures can create conflict. In order to establish common ground, you need to recognize and address gaps. It is useful to define each culture using the BRAVE model presented earlier and map them next to each other. Where are they not aligned? Determining these differences is critical to identifying shifts that need to be made and potential conflicts that may occur.

Leading the formation of a new academic unit can be one of the most rewarding and challenging assignments for an interim leader. Although the myriad of administrative issues to address can be overwhelming, beginning to lay the foundation for a positive culture should also receive significant attention.

Anthony inherited the task of organizing a newly formed college into a cohesive unit. As a highly respected faculty member within the unit, he was selected by the provost as the right person for the job. For the most part, the people and units comprising the new college were previously part of the same unit, so there was not a need to meld different organizational cultures. Developing the new organizational structure, policies and procedures, and so forth were arduous tasks, but the greatest challenges were twofold: (1) articulating to both internal and external stakeholders that college status came with new expectations and outcomes, and (2) working with everyone to define the new operating environment.

This challenge required a balancing act, as Anthony did not want to get so far down the road that the new, permanent dean did not have latitude to develop a plan of his or her own. He enlisted the support of the provost to reaffirm the changes in expectations accompanying the move to an academic college and worked with the leadership team and faculty to develop new performance expectations for the college and its faculty. Anthony applied for the permanent position but did not receive the offer; his success in moving the college out of its comfort zone may have had an adverse impact on his ability to secure the permanent position.

This example serves to illustrate one of the vagaries of interim leadership—the possibility of alienating members of the organization as a result of taking on difficult issues. Anthony did what was necessary for the good of the new college and is owed a huge debt of gratitude, but that outcome may have been achieved at a high personal cost. Not surprisingly, Anthony went on to do great things in other administrative roles.

Status Quo Interim

This scenario pushes against the primary theme of this book—taking advantage of the interim period to move the organization forward—but there are rare circumstances when aggressive, results-focused leadership is not recommended. In these cases, the interim is restricted in opportunities to lead advancement in various facets of the organization—e.g., programmatic, fiscal, or personnel—taking on the role of a manager rather than a leader.

WHAT QUALITIES MAKE A GOOD INTERIM LEADER?

In general, all the qualities that make a good leader also apply to the interim leader. However, there are a few characteristics that are particularly critical for interims:

- **Experienced**—experience provides credibility. It also allows leaders to quickly assess complex organizational situations, not just administrative matters—e.g., budget—but organizational dynamics, culture, and so on.

- **Selfless**—interim leaders must be motivated to serve the organization, and therefore need to check their egos at the door. Since a key role is to pave the way for the next leader, they need to possess the attitude, "It's not about me, it's about the organization" (Zaniello 2019).

- **Excellent communicator and collaborator**—communication is always important, but it is particularly true for interim leaders who must listen well and quickly establish relationships with those within the unit as well as with external stakeholders.

- **Courageous**—as noted above, an interim executive position comes with its own set of challenges, some of which you have not experienced before. In addition, sometimes the role requires informing the governing board or supervisor of things they might not want to hear. Interim leaders must possess the courage and resolve to take on difficult situations in a timely manner.

- **Good administrative instincts**—as noted above, interim leaders need to be able to assess situations quickly, but they also need the confidence to process this information and respond. There is no room for paralysis-by-analysis decision-making in an interim role. Successful interim leaders have the confidence to act on these instincts.

- **Personality and administrative style that fits the opportunity**—it is critical that the administrative style of the interim leader selected for the position fits the opportunity. A sure way to collapse an organization is to bring an aggressive change agent into an interim role when the unit is not prepared for change. Discussions with current and past presidents and provosts revealed this issue to be one that is sometimes neglected by appointing authorities.

Each of these qualities will be referenced repeatedly throughout this book, both in the discussion of specific interim leadership skills and activities and their demonstration in the various cases developed from interviews of past and present leaders.

WHERE DO WE FIND PEOPLE TO FILL THESE ROLES?

Clearly, interim leadership is not for everyone, and a prerequisite for success is finding a willing leader whose experience and qualities fit the opportunity at hand. Interim executives are appointed from positions both within and outside the organization. Within the organization, interims are typically identified by elevating someone from the next level down. For example, provosts or vice presidents are typically tagged to serve as interim presidents, department chairs often take on the role of interim dean, and associate or assistant vice presidents are often elevated to serve as interim vice presidents.

Interim executive leaders can also be accessed from areas external to the unit but within the university. This practice is generally not optimal, but it sometimes occurs when no one within the unit is prepared to fill the void or when internal politics prevent elevating one member over others. An example is the appointment of an associate dean from another college within the university to serve as interim dean. Recent retirees are an additional talent pool that has been tapped to fill interim executive roles.

Interim leaders are sometimes brought in from outside the university. While this practice is not employed in higher education as much as other sectors—e.g., the not-for-profit sector—there are circumstances when this option should be considered. For example, perhaps no one within the existing unit is prepared to fill the void or conflict exists such that an outside perspective is needed. Beginning a position of academic leadership can be challenging under any circumstances, but those challenges increase exponentially when you're hired into an institution from the outside. There are several executive search firms that specialize in the placement of interim leaders and have a stable of candidates prepared to step into leadership positions to allow for the smooth transition to a permanent leader (BIE Executive 2014).

Interviewed interim leaders who were hired with the assistance of an executive search firm noted that the most difficult challenge in these circumstances was quickly gaining an understanding of the institutional culture. These people tend to have experience at multiple institutions and, hence, are skilled at sorting out these situations. Interim leaders hired from outside the university all spoke to the importance of quickly establishing trust with their team. Naturally, interims who are not known are viewed with suspicion as outsiders.

A non-exhaustive media search of appointment announcements of interim presidents and provosts during the 2019 calendar year revealed forty-nine interim president appointments and sixty-three interim provost appointments at four-year institutions. Interim presidents came from a variety of positions, including retired administrators, administrators within the institution (principally provost, vice president, or dean), industry leaders, and trustees. Current administrators accounted for a little over half of the appointments, followed by retired administrators (25 percent). Interim provosts were largely pulled from within the institution, with members of the provost's leadership team and deans comprising about two-thirds of the appointments. Interim deans were largely appointed from positions within the college—most frequently associate deans, department chairs, or directors.

Of course, the circumstances and expectations of the situation should inform the choice of an interim leader. The availability of leadership within normal succession will play a large factor in choosing a strategy. Also, things such as the organizational health of the unit, prevailing challenges, ongoing major initiatives, and the goals to be achieved during the interim period will influence selection. Unfortunately, options are limited in many situations, so the leader making the selection must weigh the trade-offs carefully.

An underappreciated issue in making interim executive leader appointments from within the organization is the potential holes that are created down the organization when pulling someone up into an interim leadership role. This domino effect needs to be considered when selecting an interim leader.

Succession planning is one of the most neglected activities in higher education administration. Failure to plan for the ultimate departure of an executive leader can lead to extended transition periods that stymie forward progress.

Gardner, a former interim president, reflected on the void created when he was elevated to the position from his provost role and needed to appoint an interim provost. The dean who looked like the obvious choice for the interim role was not selected because he led the largest and most complex college. The college was going through some important transitions and lacked a capable associate dean to move into the interim dean role. In this case, the benefit-cost analysis (where costs were the risks associated with pulling the dean from the college for a year) led to the selection of an alternative interim provost. The interim provost selected had developed a deep leadership team comprised of three capable associate deans. It was clear that her college was more likely to run smoother and move forward in her absence.

This situation points to the need for developing leadership within your team and for succession planning. The dean who was not selected had been denied an opportunity due to his failure to develop a logical successor.

Chapter 2

EXECUTING THE TRANSITION

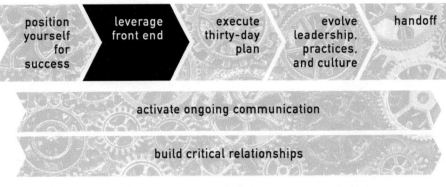

Figure 2.1. Interim Leadership Timeline, Stage 2: Leverage the Front End

The best gift an outgoing leader can give the organization is a smooth and thoughtful transition. In cases where this occurs, the initial challenges faced by the interim leader are mitigated significantly. Unfortunately, as noted in the previous chapter, sometimes circumstances prevail where this does not occur, and the new leader must work extra hard both before the first day on the job as well as in the weeks that follow.

Like most things in life, one's success in an interim position can be greatly improved through preparation. Critical to this preparation is making certain that you and your new boss are on the same page about the terms and expectations of the position. Valuable preparation can also occur in assimilating information, assessing the status of the organization, and beginning the process of building key relationships that will be important during the interim period.

STEPS FOR MAKING A SMOOTH AND THOUGHTFUL TRANSITION

When an executive leader departs, there is naturally a heightened sense of anxiety and uncertainty within an organization. Some of the questions that colleagues may have are: Who will lead during the period when new permanent leadership is being sought? How long will this period last? Will there be a dramatic change in the vision or organizational structure? Team members will also have anxiety about the future of key initiatives and projects they may be working on. Developing a clear transition plan and articulating it to all members of the organization in a timely manner can go a long way toward reducing this anxiety and preventing the rumor mill from starting to churn.

A smooth transition starts with the supervisor who is making the decisions about current and future leadership of the organization. The best transitions include a timeline and detailed process for moving to permanent leadership. The timeline should include a communications strategy, naming a transition team, securing an interim leader, and outlining a search process. These steps serve to reduce the uncertainty of people within the organization and increase accountability so that the process proceeds in a timely manner and stays on track.

A useful transition strategy that is sometimes possible is to provide overlap between the outgoing leader and the incoming interim leader. This overlap can be a valuable time for the interim leader to gain a better feel for the day-to-day operations of the position and obtain critical insights into ongoing activities of the organization. Written documentation provided by the outgoing leader outlining major initiatives, current projects, upcoming opportunities, and ongoing challenges can also provide a valuable resource for an interim leader. Of course, the possibility of taking these approaches depends on the timetable and circumstances of the outgoing leader's departure.

Setting Expectations

As noted in the previous chapter, it is critical to set expectations with your supervisor or governing board prior to stepping into the interim role. What are the specific responsibilities of the role? What are the desired outcomes during the period? What level of managerial freedom can be exercised in leading the organization? It is far easier to maintain the vision if it is made clear prior to the transition.

Interviews with previous interim leaders revealed that role ambiguity was one of the most significant challenges faced during their time as interim administrators. For example, less than half of those who served as interim deans felt that they received clear directions from the provost about goals and objectives for the interim period. It is insufficient to receive general instructions such as, "Keep the college moving forward," or a position description that outlines the basic responsibilities of the job. Incoming interim leaders should work with their supervisor to develop a clear guiding document that defines the transition plan, key goals for the interim period, critical outcomes to achieve, authority for making changes, and terms for relinquishing the interim role and returning to their former position.

Some or all of this information should be included in the formal appointment letter to the interim executive. A review of several appointment letters to interim leaders found them to be very generic, with few specifics. Most provided little detail about the duration of the appointment but rather employed phrases such as, "The interim dean will serve until a permanent dean is appointed." A list of important items to be included in an appointment letter or supporting documents is provided in Table 2.1.

Table 2.1. APPOINTMENT LETTER OR SUPPORTING DOCUMENTATION ITEMS

✓ Specific responsibilities of the position
✓ Duration (appointment date, ending date)
✓ Process and considerations for extending the appointment beyond ending date, if necessary
✓ Compensation
✓ Terms for returning to former role
✓ Resources allocated to assist in transition and execution during interim period
✓ Supervisory relationships
✓ Critical outcomes to be achieved during interim period
✓ Administrative authority and latitude .

It is insufficient that the interim and the supervisor or board be in alignment. It is vital that the supervisor or board also clearly communicates expectations of the interim leader to everyone within the organization. This communication will provide the interim leader with greater credibility and can be helpful in reinforcing goals to be achieved during the interim period.

Of course, expectations are a two-way street. It is important that you clarify what you expect from your supervisor. How frequent would you want to check in, and what form would these check-ins take? What will be their response if members of the organization who are not on board with direction from the interim leader come to them with concerns. An overwhelming piece of advice given by interim leaders was: make sure that your superior has your back. This issue will be discussed in greater detail in chapter 9.

Avoiding Transition Traps

Executives in new positions sometimes exhibit several behaviors that can lead to stumbles during the initial months. A survey of business leaders conducted by Genesis Advisers, the *Harvard Business Review*, and the International Institute of Management Development identified several of these transition traps, including:

- **Sticking with what you know**—rarely will previous competencies provide a new leader with the knowledge needed to be successful in a new role. New and focused learning is required. The importance of developing a learning plan to guide these activities is discussed later in this chapter.

- **Taking action too quickly**—a desire to establish oneself as an action-oriented leader may prompt a new administrator to move forward without adequately understanding the issues and culture of the organization. Remember, culture trumps strategy every time, so it is important to understand these aspects of the organizational climate.

- **Attempting to do too much**—the new leader moves forward in too many directions, launching many new initiatives, causing confusion within the organization, and lacking sufficient resources to allocate to so many priorities.

- **Coming in with the answer**—failing to listen and learn, the new leader reaches conclusions too quickly about critical problems and their solutions.

- **Inadequate learning**—the new leader focuses learning on the wrong things, such as the technical aspects of the organization's work, and fails to invest in learning about the organization's history, team culture, and group dynamics.

Falling into one or more of these traps can lead to a cycle of ineffectiveness during the initial months of your appointment as an interim leader (Figure 2.2). For example, inadequate learning, ineffective relationship building, and/or failing to build supportive networks can lead to bad decision-making, which results in lost credibility, eroding confidence, and resistance from team members. This outcome can translate into reduced opportunities to understand and improve relationships and networks, resulting in additional bad decisions and reduced credibility. The resulting cycle of ineffectiveness becomes difficult to break once it starts.

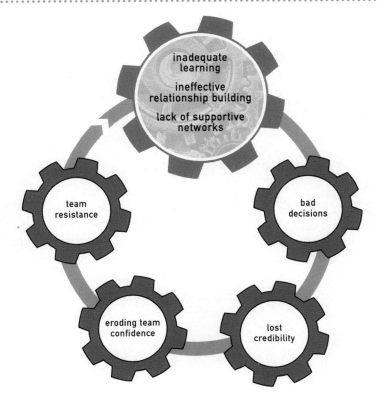

Figure 2.2. Cycle of Ineffectiveness for New Leaders

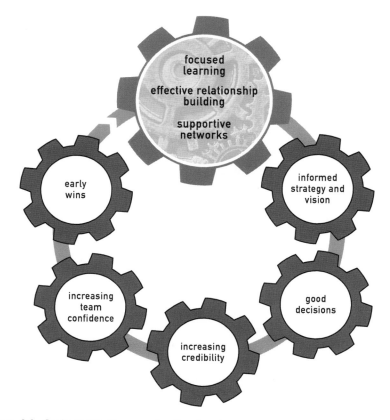

Figure 2.3. Cycle of Effectiveness for New Leaders

Conversely, the cycle of effectiveness (Figure 2.3) is rooted in investing adequately in learning and relationship building. This investment of time and energy leads to good initial decisions, increased credibility, and growing confidence of the team. Positive momentum feeds off itself, resulting in improved team performance. Recommendations throughout this chapter and in chapters 3 and 4 are focused on providing you with the tool set to avoid the cycle of ineffectiveness and jump on and stay on the cycle of effectiveness.

LEVERAGING THE FRONT END

Many leaders fall into the trap of thinking that leadership begins their first day on the job. (Bradt, Check, and Lawler 2016). Like it or not, a new leader's role (including an interim's) begins as soon as that person is identified as the one filling the position. Everything new leaders do and say and don't do and don't say will send powerful signals, starting well before they walk in the door on day one.

We will refer to the time period between accepting a position and the first day on the job as the front end. It is important to take advantage of this valuable period and leverage the front end to the greatest extent possible. New leaders who miss the opportunity to get a head start will be playing catch-up from their start date.

Of course, there are other demands on the incoming leader's time during the front end. Equally important to preparing for the new assignment is taking care of business in one's current unit. It is the outgoing leader's responsibility to develop a transition plan and assure a smooth transition for incoming leadership. These two tasks—transition out and transitioning in—need to be balanced and will represent a large time commitment.

One subtle way of creating time is to extend the start date. If there's flexibility—which is not always the case—you might negotiate a longer front end and, therefore, more time for helpful activities before day one.

Important Activities for the Front End

There are several critical activities that should be initiated prior to day one. Most of these will not be completed before the start date but instead are initiated in the front end and continued throughout the first few weeks in the new position.

1. **Identify your key stakeholders.**

   These stakeholders are people within and outside the organization who can have the greatest impact on your success in this new role. This is an exercise in prioritization. You cannot meet with everyone, so you need to be strategic in identifying and prioritizing these stakeholders.

   Many transitioning executives fail to think through this process or look in only one direction to find their key stakeholders (Bradt, Check, and Lawler 2016). "Up stakeholders" may include your boss, your indirect boss if there is a matrix organization, your boss's boss, the board of directors, or anyone else who resides further up in the organization. "Across stakeholders" might include key allies, peers, or partners who reside at the same level as the interim position within the institution's organizational chart. "Down stakeholders" usually include direct reports and other critical support people who are essential to successful implementation of your team's goals.

Your new executive assistant and other support staff should be high on this list because they have the best inside view of the position's recent history, ongoing projects, upcoming activities, and potential land mines. Quickly establishing trust and open communication with these team members will assist in the continued smooth day-to-day functioning of the organization. This is an important outcome, as nothing can adversely impact confidence in new leadership faster than the failure of rather mundane things, such as administrative approvals or reimbursements being held up and stymying progress.

Also consider former stakeholders. If you're getting promoted from within or making a lateral move, make sure to consider the up, across, and down stakeholders from your former position. Connecting with them will prove valuable if you return to that position.

2. Jump-start key relationships.

A theme throughout this book is the importance to interim leaders of establishing and continually developing key relationships with stakeholders. It is vital to prioritize your communications with stakeholders during the front end based on urgency and order of importance. These might include your boss (or chair of the board of directors), critical peers, and critical direct reports.

Conduct prestart meetings and phone calls as soon as possible. Some people entering new positions are reluctant to do this, but the value is incalculable. The outgoing leader, if still present, should be kept informed about your front end activities and may well be a valuable resource in identifying key stakeholders and facilitating conversations.

Initial meetings need not be detailed but can be used to establish a more productive and personal one-on-one relationship. Listen more than you talk during these meetings, establishing a reputation as someone who is willing to learn from colleagues as opposed to someone who is coming in with all the answers. Remember, first impressions are important and have a lasting impact on how people judge subsequent information.

These meetings can also serve a critical purpose in reducing the stress and anxiety others may experience as you assume leadership. During these meetings, you can start communicating and trying out your entry message. You can also use them to break down any rumors or false-hoods about the direction you intend to take the unit or organization.

3. **Assimilate information.**
Executive leadership positions can have big learning curves. While you aren't going to know everything about the position on day one, it is impor-tant to begin the process of assimilating information about the unit prior to your arrival. You don't want to show up on the first day and have no idea what the organization's culture looks like, what the major challenges are, what strategies are in play, or what questions you should ask. This preparation will allow you to have the greatest impact during your first thirty days.

Three areas to pay particular attention to during the front end period are the working environment, organization performance, and history.

- The working environment includes how members of the organization work with one another and how the organization interacts with others. Of course, the organization's culture is an important component of the work environment, and the BRAVE model described in chapter 1 can be used to organize your information assimilation in this area.

- Assessing organizational performance requires digging below the obvious and gaining a deeper understanding of fiscal, programmatic, and personnel performance; challenges and opportunities; and so on. Chapters 5 through 8 provide insights into assessing the organiza-tion's administrative, fiscal, and programmatic performance.

- History (at least recent history) is important. General James Mattis told me during a delightful face-to-face lunch meeting a few years ago that history was the most important subject for aspiring leaders to study. His point—understanding history provides important context in shaping your plans and helps you avoid repeating past mistakes. Obtaining multiple perspectives on recent successes, failures, issues, and priorities for the organization provides useful information with which to frame the current situation.

An important means of gathering information is through conversations with the stakeholders noted above. Conversations before you assume the position are sometimes easier because a different power dynamic exists. Try to keep the conversations forward-looking; it is not a productive use of your time to allow people to focus on the past and vent about problems with past leadership. It is important to be interested in hearing what people have to say but collect different perspectives and avoid making early commitments. The very person who sounds so reasonable in your first conversations may be the person who, a few months later, is clearly the one who gave you the worst advice.

If you have the luxury, consult with the person leaving the position. Many new leaders are reluctant to reach out, but there is no one who has more knowledge of the position's opportunities and challenges.

Seek advice from those who have been through similar circumstances. When Dr. Elson S. Floyd, president of Washington State University, passed away and I was asked to assume the role of interim president, I sought advice from a former colleague who had been through the same situation at another university. His insights about some of the unique aspects of taking up the mantle following the death of a popular leader were extremely helpful in navigating a tumultuous first thirty days.

Reports, policies, budgets, financial statements, and other documents are the second major source of information to access prior to day one. A word of warning—don't invite new team members to send you documentation unless you provide some ground rules. I found it useful to control the flow of information by asking for specific documents and formats. If you leave it to the individuals within the unit, they will overwhelm you with information and you will spend an inordinate amount of time sorting through a mountain of documents to determine what is important. One useful strategy is to ask for tightly written (two- to three-page) summaries from the internal stakeholders you have identified as most critical to learn from. These summaries can provide excellent preparation prior to some of those initial meetings referenced above. If you desire additional information about a particular topic, you can always request it.

4. Craft your entry message.

Before you start talking to any of your stakeholders, you'll want to clarify your initial message. The key piece of advice is to keep it simple. Everything you do communicates and will inform and influence your interactions with people after you start. There is much to communicate, but staging is critical. Including too much information in your initial message can lead to confusion and might communicate that you are coming in with all the answers.

Finally, if you are using it, dump the reluctant leader act. I have witnessed several interims messaging that they really didn't want the job but were "taking one for the team." This messaging will hamper credibility and the ability to effect change. Message that you are excited about the opportunity, ready to go, and looking forward to meeting everyone on the team.

5. Invest in onboarding.

Most universities have onboarding programs for people assuming executive leadership roles. Unfortunately, sometimes onboarding is reserved for permanent hires. Request a formal onboarding process, which typically includes an onboarding coach. Granted, the onboarding process is likely to be shorter and less comprehensive than those designed for permanent hires, but it can still provide enormous value. Onboarding meetings can be a useful activity to assimilate information and develop stakeholder relationships.

If the interim leader is coming from within the institution, there is a tendency for some to think that onboarding is not necessary. This is untrue, as new norms and cultures exist across organizations within the same institution. Some might think, "Well, I know her—there is no need for any type of onboarding session," but it is important to check in with key stakeholders and establish a new relationship based on your new position.

Only about half of the interim leaders surveyed had any form of formal onboarding process. Those who engaged in onboarding found the process helpful. For example, the interim deans surveyed found that assignment of a peer coach to check in with (typically a fellow dean) proved to be of significant value. An executive leadership position can be a lonely job, so developing this support network is critical.

6. Identify land mines.

The front end period is a good time to begin the process of identifying land mines. These are issues that can short-circuit your leadership during the first few months. Land mines always exist, but they are most easily hidden from you leading up to day one and over the first thirty days.

Knowing where land mines may exist and learning how to navigate around them will allow you to avoid their potential adverse consequences.

Land mines are not easy to recognize; if they were, they would not be land mines. Conversations with key stakeholders can be a first step to identifying them. Typically, you cannot simply ask, "Where are the land mines?" However, you can probe with intentional questions. Land mines can take a variety of forms; some of the more prevalent sources include ongoing personnel issues, organizational structure that is incongruent with mission, tensions between members of the leadership team, and sacred cows that have generated controversy in the past.

John Maxwell (2011) stresses that land mines can sometimes be self-induced. This important category of land mines can result from personal behaviors that undermine your leadership. A tendency to micromanage, be overly critical, or overanalyze situations are all examples of self-inflicted land mines.

7. Begin to learn the organizational language.

Colleges and universities not only have their own unique culture, but they also have their own organizational language. A challenge new leaders invariably encounter is learning the seemingly secret code that people within an organization employ daily. Even if you are coming from another unit within the same university, there is still some language specific to the new unit that needs to be learned.

This challenge is particularly daunting for leaders coming to positions from outside the university. Colleges and universities have their own labels and acronyms that are not shared by other institutions. The problem is that many administrators and staff don't know that they are speaking a coded language. New leaders can get lost in conversations as they try to translate these terms. It is like trying to follow a complex conversation in a language in which you are not fluent.

One of the most helpful onboarding resources we developed when I was serving as provost was a glossary of terms, abbreviations, and acronyms for new leaders. Check to see if such a resource is available; if not, it might be a resource you could ask your executive assistant to begin developing. It will also be a useful resource for the incoming permanent leader.

8. Get your personal affairs and office setup in place.

You don't want to spend your initial days on the job unpacking your office or filling out appointment paperwork. Get as many of these personal affairs as possible completed prior to your start date. Work with the executive assistant to develop a list of everything that needs to get done and turn him or her loose to complete those tasks.

9. Establish a clear breakpoint.

As discussed in the previous chapter, it is important not to carry your current role into your new one. This can be difficult for interim leaders who are filling a position within the same institution. Nonetheless, it is important to establish a clear breakpoint, perhaps over a weekend, when you mentally end one position and start the other. The new position will require you to think and act differently, so making this mental break will allow you avoid mixing the two roles.

A helpful checklist of front end activities is provided in Table 2.2.

Table 2.2. CHECKLIST OF "FRONT END" ACTIVITIES

✓ Negotiate clear expectations and terms of appointment with supervisor

✓ Develop transition plan for exiting previous position

✓ Initiate meetings with key members of leadership team

✓ Collect and begin analyzing available documents

✓ Develop list of key internal and external stakeholders

✓ Request additional documents to supplement those initially provided

✓ Assess organizational culture and performance

✓ Consult with outgoing leader

✓ Craft early message to organization

✓ Draft thirty-day plan

✓ Meet with key support staff—e.g., executive assistant, chief financial officer

✓ Consult with colleagues in similar roles

✓ Get personal affairs and office setup in place

✓ Work with supervisor to develop an onboarding plan

MAKING THE ANNOUNCEMENT

The strategy for making the announcement of the interim appointment will depend significantly on the position being filled and the circumstances that have created the need for an interim leader. For interim presidents, the announcement will require a well-thought-out rollout with a significant external component. For more internally focused positions—e.g., most vice president positions—the announcement can be much simpler and directed toward internal stakeholders.

The announcement of an interim executive appointment should come from the president or provost. In addition to announcing the appointment and introducing the new leader, the communication should reaffirm the transition plan to permanent leadership, including the anticipated length of the interim period and the process for identifying a new leader. The announcement should also affirm the interim leader's authority and state any important goals and outcomes desired for the interim period.

The phasing of the initial communication is important. Members of the leadership team should receive the first communication, followed by a comprehensive announcement to all members of the organization. A press release should be prepared for distribution immediately after hitting send on the comprehensive announcement.

For more externally focused positions, such as president and some deans, careful consideration should be given to the public phase of the announcement. Pre-calls should be made to important donors, public officials, and alumni to assure they are not blindsided by the announcement. Key press outlets can be contacted beforehand to provide a heads-up that an announcement is forthcoming. Some news media will desire access to the new interim president immediately after the announcement. Additional discussion of developing this communication plan is provided in chapter 3, "Developing Your Thirty-Day Plan."

Chapter 3

DEVELOPING YOUR THIRTY-DAY PLAN

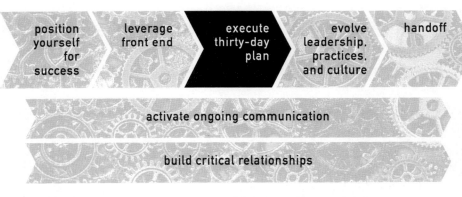

Figure 3.1. Interim Leadership Timeline, Stage 3: Execute Thirty-Day Plan

An important activity during the front end period is developing a thirty-day plan. Leadership articles and books often talk about creating a one-hundred-day plan to guide the initial months in a new position. With an interim role, everything is compressed. Interim executives need to master short-term planning, an uncommon skill in colleges and universities that tend to be focused on longer-term planning. Interim leaders should develop a thirty-day plan.

PREPARING THE THIRTY-DAY PLAN

The majority of interim leaders interviewed did not have a formal, written plan when they began their new position. Those who did seem to have had a smoother transition. Many who did not soon recognized the need for one and developed a plan during the initial weeks of their tenure.

The thirty-day plan not only provides structure and meaning to the first month in your new position, but it also provides a framework to build on for developing a more comprehensive plan covering the entire transition period and beyond. When developing a thirty-day plan, it is important to keep deliverables for the period of interim service top-of-mind. It is easy to get caught in the mode of solving each daily crisis and not achieving the desired outcomes. A plan allows you to communicate these outcomes to the team and keeps you and the team focused and accountable throughout the transition period.

Some essential elements of a thirty-day plan include:

- Goals mapped to various points on the interim leadership timeline, and a plan for measuring these goals and tracking success;

- Identification of key stakeholders with whom to build critical relationships (see chapter 2);

- An onboarding plan to assist in building critical relationships and assimilating information (see chapter 2);

- A preliminary assessment of the organization's culture, working environment, and performance developed during the front end, and a plan to continue the current discernment process;

- A resource scan of the availability and allocation of human, financial, and physical resources relative to the goals at hand;

- A communication plan to guide messaging to both internal and external stakeholders;

- A learning and professional development plan to acquire the knowledge and skills necessary to lead the organization and achieve your own professional development goals; and

- An action plan to define activities during the first thirty days that set the trajectory for the entire interim period.

There is no magic format for the thirty-day plan. Whatever content and format best fit your needs will probably serve you best. The outline in Table 3.1 provides a sample structure.

....

Table 3.1. SAMPLE THIRTY-DAY PLAN OUTLINE

Organizational Assessment:

- Culture (behaviors, relationships, attitudes, values, environment)
- Working environment
- Organizational performance

Jump-start Key Relationships:

- Meetings
- Phone calls

Key Stakeholders:

- Internal
- External

Communication Plan:

- Initial message
- Following (phased) messages

New Leader Assimilation:

- Meetings
- Primary messages

Information Assimilation:

- Additional assimilation activities
- Issues requiring additional investigation

Team Assessment:

- Team culture and performance
- Diversity, equity, and inclusion assessment
- Individual assessments

Learning Plan:

- Onboarding activities
- Key questions to address

Specifying Goals and Outcomes

Simply listing outcomes that are desired by the conclusion of the interim period is not adequate and will not provide the necessary structure to maximize success. It is useful to map these goals over the period of service in the interim position. There are goals that need to be accomplished for a smooth transition from the previous leader to the interim. Other goals must be accomplished to continue advancing ongoing projects and initiatives. In addition, your boss likely has articulated some goals to be accomplished during your time of service. Finally, there are new goals identified by you and your team to advance the organization through the transition period and beyond. Mapping these goals at various points along the interim leadership timeline is a useful means of organizing your plan.

ASSESSING THE CURRENT STATUS OF THE ORGANIZATION

A critical part of the thirty-day plan includes the steps required to continue the assessment process begun during the front end. The primary objective of the first thirty days is to seek to understand.

Meet with your team members, individually and in groups, to gain insight into their needs and priorities for the interim period. Use these meetings to gain a deeper understanding of various aspects of the organization—its mission, culture, values, and strategies. Continue to build on the relationships that you initiated during the front end. Again, if you were promoted from within the organization, you will have a good handle on much of this information, although it is still important to assimilate information in the context of your new role.

One-on-one meetings with members of the leadership team should occur as soon as possible. It is helpful to employ a standardized approach to these meetings to enable you to collect consistent information. Certain questions should be asked of all team members, enabling you to assess consistency and commitment to mission, values, and so on. Sometimes what people don't say is more revealing than what they say.

As you continue your assessment, you will begin to gain understanding of your new team's capabilities and internal dynamics. Some strategies and tactics useful in deepening this understanding of your new team members and moving them forward on a successful path are provided in chapter 5, "Working with Your New Team."

In addition to assessing the functionality of the team as a group and its individual members' capabilities, your organizational assessment should evaluate the workplace environment. Build upon the BRAVE culture assessment and dig deeper into the functioning of the team. Be on the lookout for signs of a hostile work environment and whether individual members of the team are devalued, marginalized, or even harassed.

In recent times, there has been an increasing imperative for colleges and universities to better promote diversity, inclusion, and access in the workplace. Justifiably, you will be asked to provide leadership in this area and promote a more diverse, equitable, and inclusive work environment. A reasonable goal for the first thirty days is to complete a preliminary assessment of the workplace culture, practices, and processes to identify any existing issues that might violate the institution's principles on diversity, equity, and inclusion. Included in this assessment is determining past efforts to advance these policies and whether a plan exists for the unit. If one does not exist, a major contribution of your interim period should be to begin the process of developing such a plan.

This assessment should extend to the office of the interim. For example, the interim may assume that everything is okay even though there are underlying issues that could include bullying, harassment, and so on by individuals who seem loyal and helpful to the interim. It might be useful to obtain some external feedback to ensure that you aren't missing anything due to your own blind spots. A discussion of assessing and advancing diversity, equity, and inclusion in the workplace is provided in chapter 5.

Seek to understand the organization's overall strategy and the key short-term and long-term goals. What major initiatives are being executed to deliver on these goals? What progress is being made on these initiatives? Identify strengths and weaknesses of the organization that will help you formulate your next actions. Complete an inventory of current projects being conducted within the unit, including their progress and timelines for completion.

A key document in this process *could* be the organization's strategic plan. The word "could" is emphasized because, while just about all organizations have a strategic plan, they all don't actively employ the plan as a principal guiding document. If you have inherited an organization that does, the job of assessing the current status of the organization and setting a course forward will be much easier.

Astute leaders manage the budget to drive behavior and accomplish goals. To do so requires that you have a firm handle on the organization's financial condition and the budget you inherited. Are allocations consistent with the goals that have been mapped for the organization? What is the fiscal health of the organization and are immediate actions required to improve the situation? More information on assessing financial performance can be found in chapter 7, "Managing the Budget."

Remember, impermanence has value. An interim leader brings a unique level of objectivity and detachment to the position. Detachment allows you to step back, observe what's going on, and take in and assess conflicting opinions.

Conducting a Resource Scan

In addition to an assessment of the organization's workplace environment and culture, you will also want to develop an inventory of the availability and allocation of the resources available to the unit. Resources can take on a variety of dimensions, including human, financial, and physical. Are there adequate resources to achieve the goals set for the interim period? Are the resources that are available allocated appropriately?

Human resources are always the most critical resource when leading organizations within higher education. Most colleges and universities expend over 80 percent of their total budget on human capital, so it is not surprising that this area should receive the most attention. Not only should your inventory look at the quantity of staff relative to the job at hand but also the capabilities, capacity, and training of team members. Additional detail on assessing the human resources at your disposal is provided in chapter 5.

Most units within higher education institutions have a variety of revenue sources at their disposal—e.g., general operating allocation from the general university budget, development funds, capital funds, and auxiliary funds. In inventorying financial resources, it is important to identify all available funds and the various restrictions that are imposed on their use. Additional detail on inventorying the financial resources at your disposal is provided in chapter 7.

Another area that can pose significant resource challenges to an incoming executive leader is information technology. Are the appropriate data available to analyze and make critical decisions? Are the appropriate software tools available, and are sufficient staff trained in their use? It is not uncommon for a new leader to come into a unit and want to analyze a particular situation or area, only to be hamstrung by inadequate data resources to conduct the appropriate analysis.

Developing a Communication Plan

An important element of the thirty-day plan is the communication plan. A primary theme of this book is communicate, communicate, and communicate. Executive leaders in higher education can't communicate enough, and this adage is particularly true for those in interim positions. Communicate up and down the organization, and within and outside the organization.

In your communication efforts, repetition is essential. Jeff Weiner, CEO of LinkedIn, remarked in an interview, "If you want to get your point across, especially to a broader audience, you need to repeat yourself so often, you get sick of hearing yourself say it. And only then will people begin to internalize what you're saying" (Blodget 2014). A study of managers in the workplace by Professors Tsedal Neely of Harvard and Paul Leonardi of Northwestern found a simple truth: "Managers who were deliberately redundant moved their projects forward faster and more smoothly" (Neeley and Leonardi 2011).

Communication plans need to be flexible and responsive to issues that emerge, but the thirty-day plan should be ready for launch on day one of your appointment. Don't try to deliver the entirety of your message in one communication. Focus on simplifying the message. Colin Powell explained it this way: "Great leaders are almost always great simplifiers, who can cut through argument, debate, and doubt to offer a solution everybody can understand" (Harari 2002). Effective leaders talk to their people in language they understand and use language that is free of jargon and technical-speak. Correctly communicating the vision and direction of the organization reduces doubt and debate and provides clarity for stakeholders.

The thirty-day communication plan should not only focus on your plans for the organization but should also allow members of the organization to know you as a leader and a human being. One cannot overstate the importance of this messaging in reducing anxiety among team members.

The thirty-day plan should be structured in phases where messages build upon previous communications but continue to reinforce the primary initial points. As discussed in chapter 2, the first message to the organization should be sent prior to your first day on the job; it should be followed with a message that is ready for distribution on day one. Unless the circumstances require immediate intervention, go slowly in the first thirty days. You are still converging, still listening and learning.

These two communications and others in the first thirty days are critical in defining your leadership. Just as people draw first impressions from initial meetings, they also develop impressions from initial electronic or written communications. You are in the honeymoon phase of your appointment, so take advantage of it. People are more likely to pay attention to a message from the new leader during this time (or at least read or listen to it). But remember, everything is compressed during a period of interim leadership, including the honeymoon phase.

When building your internal communication plan, it is important to recognize that information voids do not remain empty. They will be filled with whatever rumors or half-truths make their way through informal communication channels. Your goal is to set a firm direction and address any concerns that may have been raised to date. It is much more effective and time efficient to avoid these occurrences than to try refuting false information once it has already made its way across the organization. A comprehensive communication plan can minimize this behavior.

Your communication strategy should utilize every means possible—face-to-face meetings, news media, written correspondence, email, social media, and so on. Do not rely strictly on electronic communications. Too often, when information voids occur, a common response of the leader responsible is, "I don't understand—I sent out an email." This is the byproduct of a communication strategy that is over-reliant on a single medium.

You cannot do this alone. If you have a communications unit, developing and executing a communication plan should be its number one priority. Work with your immediate reports to assure that you have agreement on a message and they are supporting your talking points.

If your organization has multiple locations, it is critical to get out and visit these sites. Distance has a way of further isolating people. There is no substitute for face-to-face presence; if the number of locations is not too numerous, it is helpful to visit them within the first thirty days.

Make certain that the communication plan includes steps to be taken to message external stakeholders, including donors, alumni, business and industry leaders, and policy makers who interact with the organization. The main message is that the organization is in good hands and moving forward in a positive direction. Consider the network of stakeholders identified in the front end as you specifically determine your target audiences and tailor your message. Modify the communiqué for your various audiences while maintaining the core message. Communications with key external stakeholders will be covered in more detail in chapter 8, "Managing External Relations."

Developing a Learning Plan

Any successful transition requires dedicating time and energy to learning about the organization; when a new leader fails, a failure to learn effectively is almost certainly a factor. Few new leaders take the time to think systematically about their learning priorities. Having the discipline to prepare a learning plan will provide the necessary structure to this important activity.

The first step in developing a learning plan is to determine what is most important to learn about the new organization. Planning to learn means determining in advance what the important questions are and how you can best answer them. Information assimilation and other activities completed in the front end should be helpful in making these determinations. Next, you need to climb the learning curve as quickly as possible. The more quickly and efficiently you learn, the sooner you will be able to close the window of vulnerability that accompanies starting any new position.

During the initial months of your service, you will almost certainly identify some areas of the job where you possess serious knowledge and experience gaps. These gaps are inevitable, as it is impossible to be fully prepared to lead in all areas of the new position. No one expects you to know everything required to do the job, and you should not feel deficient or vulnerable as a result of these gaps. I found the best approach is to study the area, develop questions, and simply ask for assistance from knowledgeable colleagues. The learning plan should be constantly updated as these gaps are identified.

Early in the transition, you will inevitably feel as if you are drinking from a fire hose. There is so much information coming at you, most of it unfiltered, that it is easy to miss what is important. The learning plan can help you organize and prioritize information to minimize this feeling. Of course, learning during a transition is a dynamic process. At first your learning agenda will consist mostly of questions, but as you begin addressing these questions, new issues and required information will reveal itself.

Watkins (2013) cautions that new leaders can suffer from the action imperative, a malady whose primary symptom is a near-compulsive need to take action. New leaders believe they are too busy to devote time to systematic learning and need to show their team that they are action-oriented. Being too busy to learn can result in a death spiral in which, if you do not learn, you can easily make poor early decisions that undermine your credibility, making people less likely to share important information with you, leading to more bad decisions (see Figure 2.2). To remain on the Cycle of Effectiveness (Figure 2.3), it is therefore imperative for you to balance learning with the other critical tasks of the position.

DEFINING YOUR LEADERSHIP APPROACH

The thirty-day plan should be framed by your initial thinking about the leadership approach you will employ during the initial phase of the

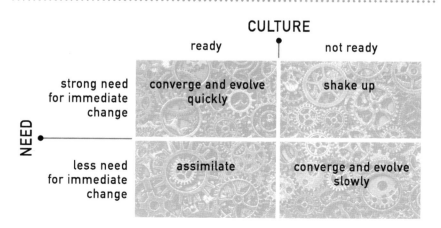

Figure 3.2. Leadership Approach Based upon Need and Readiness for Change

interim appointment. Obviously, that approach will be significantly influenced by the context and culture you face, as identified by your initial organizational assessment.

Bradt, Check, and Lawler (2016) have an interesting typology for classifying the situation a new leader might face based on the organization's need and readiness for change. A leadership approach is then identified for each combination of need and readiness, as shown in the four-quadrant diagram (Figure 3.2).

1. **Assimilate** when your analysis indicates that urgent change is not required to deliver the expected results and yet the readiness for change exists as reflected in having a cohesive team in place. Together with your team and your stakeholders, you can figure out the minor changes that need to be made over time. This is a wonderful but rare situation. In most cases, you'll want to converge and evolve.

2. **Converge and evolve slowly** when your analysis indicates that urgent change is not required but slight adjustments will be needed over time to deliver the expected results, yet the culture is not ready to change to support the required adjustments. First, become part of the organization and then slowly start to implement the required changes.

3. **Converge and evolve quickly** when your analysis indicates that significant changes are required immediately to deliver expected results and the culture is ready for change. You may be the catalyst that helps the organization wake up to the urgent need for change.

The "Converge and Evolve Quickly" scenario provides an opportunity to lead with an action imperative. Having a culture that is ready for change does not mean that change will be embraced by all; it simply means that the environment is present such that resistance can be managed and success achieved.

Fiona, a former interim dean, inherited a problematic situation where her predecessor did not adequately hold members of the organization accountable. Faculty and staff were routinely violating university and college policies, and unit leaders were not held accountable for spending in excess of budgeted amounts. The lack of discipline had led to significant programmatic and fiscal breakdowns.

During her initial meeting with the provost, he specifically asked her to address growing concerns about the academic and fiscal performance of the college. Fiona requested that the provost attend a college leadership team meeting to reinforce the need for change. Although some faculty were antagonistic with one another and against the new leadership's call for greater accountability, there was general agreement that change was necessary if the college was to elevate its status within the university.

With the leadership team, the interim dean assembled performance metrics and met one-on-one with each faculty member (it was a relatively small college) to discuss their performance using the objective measures. Fiona also instituted a peer-review portion of the annual review process that involved an elected set of peers reviewing performance data and providing input to the dean. Taking any arguments of subjectivity or bias off the table, these steps increased individual accountability. Monthly budget reports were distributed to unit leaders, and any situations of overspending were flagged.

The college made a significant turnaround during the year of interim leadership. Fiona's recognition of a need for immediate change and a culture which could handle these dramatic steps allowed her to achieve success during this period of transition.

4. **Shake Up** when significant changes must be made immediately to deliver the expected results and the culture is not ready to change. In this scenario, you have a truly challenging and high-risk situation, and the going will be tough. Know that you may end up as the "dead hero," paving the way for your successor to complete the needed transformation.

The "Shake Up" approach is sometimes necessary to address a crisis situation. Although the organization might not be ready for change, immediate action is needed to correct dysfunction that might have catastrophic implications if continued.

A former interim vice president of student affairs, Joyce inherited a situation where the university had experienced significant issues with the management of financial aid, to the point where students were not receiving their state and federal disbursements in a timely manner. The previous semester, long lines emerged daily outside the financial aid office and university phones were lit up with parents calling to complain about the delays. Joyce was hired from outside the university due to her knowledge and experience within the area of student financial services, with the specific charge of addressing the crisis.

Within thirty days, she moved the director of student financial services to another office and assumed leadership of the financial aid office. By the end of the thirty-day period, she had developed a comprehensive plan consisting of IT solutions, process improvement, and personnel training to address the perilous situation. Financial aid distribution went much smoother the following semester and continued to improve in subsequent semesters. In this case, Joyce employed a shake-up strategy and even went so far as to take over direct management of the problem area.

LOOK FOR EARLY WINS

An important component of your thirty-day plan is the identification of some early wins. Early wins are important because they build confidence and credibility, both within the team and with others outside the team. People have faith and trust in leaders who deliver. They also communicate that you are not a status quo leader.

Work with your team to identify these early wins; there are likely some ongoing projects that can be carried to fruition. When selecting from potential early wins, the first criteria is that they are attainable. Failure to deliver will have adverse impacts similar in scope and scale to the positive impacts that a win will have. Look for accomplishments that will be appreciated by the team and will have some visibility outside the team. Also, look for early wins that demonstrate behavior that you are trying to instill in the organization. Early wins are likely not going to be major accomplishments, as they need to be achieved within the first thirty to ninety days of your tenure. They may be derived from delivering on ongoing projects that have been difficult for the team to push through the finish line. It may be necessary to invest resources in delivering on these early wins.

When an early win is achieved, it is important to celebrate the accomplishment, giving credit to the team and thus boosting their morale and confidence that the organization is moving forward. Remember, interim leadership is not about you.

> Early wins need not be monumental achievements. Sometimes small but symbolic changes can message that the transition period will be one of positive forward movement.
>
> Ryan, a former interim dean, assumed office when the previous dean decided to step down following his five-year performance review and return to the faculty. The dean had been a very divisive figure, and one faculty criticism was that he often promoted himself rather than the college. An unpopular decision the dean had made was to convert the departmental conference room to a large, lavish office for himself. A small but powerful symbolic step Ryan immediately took was to convert the dean's office back to a conference room and move his personal office to a smaller, more humble space. Actions speak louder than words, and this action communicated that the interim dean was going to do whatever was best for the college. Ryan identified a small but meaningful early win and delivered it in the first month of his appointment.

When I assumed the interim presidency of WSU, we were just concluding a seven-year development campaign and reaching our monetary goal of $1 billion. While this was a tremendous achievement for the university and we enthusiastically celebrated the milestone, it was not really an early win. It was actually an accomplishment of the previous eight years and one of the previous president's cornerstone achievements. A couple of early wins were the successful hiring of the inaugural dean for the new medical school and securing the school's first round of appropriations from the state legislature. These accomplishments communicated that we were moving forward and were capable of significant success during the remainder of the transition period.

CHECKING BACK WITH THE THIRTY-DAY PLAN

At the conclusion of the thirty-day period, it is time to check in and determine what you should keep and stop or start doing to be even more effective with your team. Evaluate whether the deliverables identified for the first thirty days were indeed met. Reevaluate your early assessment of the culture, working environment, and organizational performance based on additional information assimilated over the first thirty days. Identify any important external and internal stakeholders missed in your initial list and assess whether satisfactory progress is being made in building relationships with key stakeholders. It may be useful to complete a strengths, weaknesses, opportunities, and threats (SWOT) analysis and compare it with the current thinking of the leadership team.

This is an opportune time for new leaders to decide how they are going to evolve their strategies and practices to capitalize on changing circumstances—especially around people, plans, performance tracking, and program management. If the wrong people are on the bus or personnel issues are identified that are hampering the organization, it is time to address them (more discussion in chapter 5). As strategic issues are identified, steps should be developed to resolve them. If fiscal issues are identified in your budget assessment, action steps should be formulated to address them at this time (more discussion in chapter 7).

Developing the Next Stage Action Plan

Based on your assessment activities during the front end and first thirty days, develop a concise and clear plan for the next stage of your interim leadership period. This action plan provides an opportunity to adjust from the thirty-day plan. Transitions are fraught with risk, and leaders start with imperfect information. Some things work better than expected, and some things turn out to be harder or more complicated than expected. New leaders can't control that, but they can control how they react and adjust (Bradt 2016).

This action plan should be built collaboratively with members of your leadership team to obtain their buy-in and contributions. The action plan should be outcome-driven, with goals and milestones for specific intervals of your interim leadership period and beyond—e.g., 60-, 120-, and 180-day milestones.

Build on your entry message and thirty-day communication plan to develop a longer-term plan for communication strategies during the remainder of the interim period. Again, phasing is important, so it is helpful to plan out communication goals over the coming months. In these messages, articulate goals, describe new and ongoing initiatives, and celebrate successes. Focus not only on the *what* but also the *why*. People will appreciate knowing the rationale behind any changes that are being made. Monitor and adjust your message as appropriate on an ongoing basis.

From this point on, your job is to set direction and manage the team. This activity involves such things as structuring your own work, managing the new team, building internal and external relationships, setting strategy, managing the budget, and decision-making and change management. Each of these areas is discussed in the following five chapters.

Chapter 4

STRUCTURING YOUR WORK

In his classic *The Effective Executive*, Peter Drucker wrote that effective leaders do three things well: (1) manage their time, (2) focus on results, and (3) do first things first by concentrating on the things that matter. This three-ingredient recipe is an excellent guide for structuring work as an interim leader.

SETTING PRIORITIES

Perhaps Peter Drucker's most famous quote is, "First things first, second things not at all." The ability to set priorities, focus on them, and not deviate may be the most important skill for professional success. With limited available time and energy, there are only so many things that can be done—no matter how many time management skills you learn. And because not all things get you the same return on investment, it is important that you only do those things that are the best investment of your time, energy, and resources. This is particularly true for interim leaders who are working within a compressed time frame to deliver on goals set by themselves, the leadership team, and their boss.

If leaders let the flow of daily events determine what they engage in and what they take seriously, they will fritter away precious time and energy in day-to-day operations and accomplish little. What executive leaders need are criteria that enable them to work on the truly important, results-oriented activities, even though these activities are not always found in the natural flow of events. By focusing on limited priorities, the flow of events will become more and more influenced by those priorities, creating an organizational culture focused on generating important, results-oriented outcomes.

You should be clear about your most critical priorities in the short, medium, and longer term and identify the primary outcomes you want to achieve. These priorities should be imbedded in your thirty-day plan. Avoid the temptation to have too many priorities. A lengthy list of priorities is somewhat oxymoronic in that the items included are really not priorities at all but a wish list of unachievable outcomes. Focus on a small set of priorities with achievable and tangible outcomes.

Drucker notes that the job is not just to set priorities but to identify "posteriorities"—deciding which tasks are not going to be tackled and sticking to the decision. Setting a posteriority is often unpleasant because every posteriority is someone else's priority. Eliminating activities whose utility has run its course is not something that we do particularly well in higher education. Most colleges and universities have more than their fair share of courses and programs that are no longer of interest to enough students to justify their continuation. The same holds true for administrative activities that have passed their useful life. Nonetheless, these courses, programs, and activities continue year after year because no one has the courage to make the much-needed changes. More on this topic in chapter 6, "Decision-making and Change Management."

As noted in chapter 3, one of the first things interim leaders must do to prioritize their time is shed as many prior responsibilities as possible. It is common for people moving into interim roles to feel they can balance their new responsibilities with many of the responsibilities of their previous position. Interim executive positions are more than full-time jobs, so trying to handle the multitude of responsibilities on top of prior responsibilities is a prescription for failure. This problem appears to occur with some frequency with interim deans who may be elevated from faculty roles such as department chair, center director, or senior faculty member. Several interim deans interviewed lamented the mistake of trying to continue to teach courses, supervise graduate students, and/ or manage research projects.

GETTING CONTROL OF YOUR SCHEDULE

Academic leaders who hope to move their organization forward need to take control of their schedules, get clear about what's important, and focus on results rather than activity. For the new leader, there is no time like the present to begin this exercise. Effective leaders don't start with tasks, they start with time. Time is the limiting factor; unlike other resources, one cannot rent, hire, or buy more time. You must work systematically at managing the portion of your time that can be brought under your control.

The first step in gaining control of your time is to develop a thorough understanding of where your time is spent. As someone new to the organization, a useful starting point is to review the time allocation of your predecessor. Ask your executive assistant to pull your predecessor's last couple of monthly calendars. Where was time being allocated? What were the regular, recurring meetings that were being attended? What meetings were routinely appearing on the calendar that were not regularly scheduled? What percentage of an average workday was allocated to meetings? What were the major time demands during evenings and weekends?

A common mistake made by a new leader is to accept the routine of the predecessor as your own. There is absolutely no reason to accept the predecessor's time allocation as the appropriate one for you. You likely have a different administrative style, different skills, and different goals and priorities, all of which may dictate a different optimal time allocation.

Early in the interim period, a new leader needs blocks of time to analyze the situation and develop plans. It is critical to build these blocks of time into your schedule and try to avoid scheduling over them. If this discipline is not instituted, it will be very difficult to find work time during work hours. Relying on evenings and weekends for blocks of work time is a recipe for burnout, particularly since many executive roles have large time demands during evenings and weekends.

To provide some structure to the discussion, I decided to look at my own time allocation during my administrative appointments as a dean, interim provost, and interim president. Although the dean appointment was not interim, I used my calendar during my first year in the position as an approximation of a time allocation an interim dean might experience. By referring back to my annual calendars, I was able to assign my scheduled time during twelve random weeks in each position into fourteen broad categories. The average weekly time allocations are shown in Table 4.1. These allocations are not necessarily optimal, but they reflect what my successor would have inherited from me. Only scheduled appointments, activities, and events as shown on my daily calendar are included; therefore, short phone calls, impromptu meetings, email, work on the computer, and so on are not factored into the allocations.

Table 4.1. **AVERAGE WEEKLY TIME ALLOCATION AS INTERIM PRESIDENT, INTERIM PROVOST, AND DEAN**

	Interim President		Interim Provost		Dean	
	Hours/ week	%	Hours/ week	%	Hours/ week	%
Travel Time	5.8	12	3.5	10	3.6	9
Government Relations	4.3	9	1.1	3	1.8	4
Development and Alumni	5.9	13	2.4	7	5.4	14
External Relations	2.5	6	2.8	8	2.4	6
Own Regularly Scheduled Meetings	2.4	5	2.8	8	2.5	6
Others' Regularly Scheduled Meetings	2.4	5	2.6	7	2.8	7
One-on-one and Small Group Meetings	6.5	14	9.4	27	11.6	30
Phone Time	2.0	4	0.9	3	1.8	4
Scheduled Work Time	2.6	5	1.4	4	2.6	7
University Events	4.3	9	3.1	9	2.1	5
Governance (Board of Regents)	3.0	6	1.1	3	0.3	1
Faculty, Staff, Student Groups	1.7	4	1.4	4	0.6	2
Athletics	2.8	6	1.3	4	0.6	2
Other	1.1	2	1.0	3	1.0	3
TOTAL	**47.3**	**100%**	**34.8**	**100%**	**39.1**	**100%**

Obviously, these are three very different roles with significantly different responsibilities, and the time distributions reflect this. The expansive external role of a university president is clearly illustrated, as contrasted with the largely internal role of the provost, which is dominated by regularly scheduled meetings and one-on-ones. My dean's role was significantly more externally oriented than that of my dean colleagues; hence, the relatively large amount of time allocated to development, external relations, government relations, and travel.

The first thing to note is that the president and provost positions were interim roles and would likely differ for someone in a permanent position.

For example, a permanent president would likely spend a larger percentage of time on development. The exercise revealed that scheduled time averaged between thirty-five and forty-eight hours per week, depending on the position. While we attempted to set aside blocks of work time each week, that amount was not even remotely adequate to complete regular communications—e.g., email, written correspondence, phone calls—required for each position, nor paperwork such as completing performance reviews, reports, financials, and so on. This is the root cause of sixty- to seventy-hour workweeks, which should be avoided.

Looking at these summaries says a lot about how I spent my time and my priorities in each of the roles. The question my successor should ask is: "Does this distribution of time reflect how I should optimally allocate my time to deliver on goals for the first year of my service?"

Once you understand how your time would be allocated under the inherited schedule, you can start revising the schedule to fit your own needs. Begin with the regularly scheduled commitments and determine, one by one, whether they are an appropriate use of your time. There are two sets of scheduled meetings to take a critical look at—those you control and those you are invited or required to attend. For meetings under your control, this is not a yes or no decision, although complete elimination is certainly an option. A common modification employed by interim leaders surveyed was to change the duration or frequency of administrative meetings under their own control. For meetings you are invited to attend, you might consider sending a member of your leadership team who has a deeper knowledge and appreciation of the meeting topic. For required meetings such as those called by your boss—e.g., university leadership meetings—you don't have much choice but to pen them into your calendar.

Reorganization of the inherited schedule of meetings will not only help prioritize your time but will also communicate that the transition period is not going to be "business as usual."

An interim provost who ultimately became the permanent provost, Erika shared her response to the schedule inherited from her predecessor. After reviewing the list of meetings that she was initially scheduled to attend, she determined that many were scheduled by the provost's office and most were held weekly, with a duration of one to two hours. Following a few weeks of observing these meetings, Erika set a goal of reducing by 25 percent the time commitment for regularly scheduled meetings held by the provost's office. Over the next few weeks, the entire staff worked to inventory all meetings and then proceeded to evaluate the usefulness of each meeting as well as its frequency and duration. Meeting formats were also changed to minimize one-way information sharing. Erika admitted that the 25 percent figure was somewhat arbitrary, but it forced everyone to prioritize their time. She noted that reaching the goal was not that difficult.

While you are evaluating the usefulness of various meetings, it is appropriate to consider the composition of attendees as well. Several interims interviewed noted that the meeting schedule they inherited did not put the right set of people in the room at the appropriate frequency. Some noted past use of large meetings with a diverse array of participants, which did not provide opportunities for problem-solving and were used exclusively for information exchange. As Collins (2001) notes, it is important to get the right people on the bus and sitting in the right seats. The same logic applies to meetings; the composition should match the objective. Making some quick changes can message action and foster new communication and collaboration to move on the action plan.

Once you have carved out some large blocks of time through meeting realignment, you need to work on the next largest time allocation category—ad hoc small group and one-on-one meetings. Sit down with the person responsible for scheduling your time and develop a protocol for accepting meetings and other commitments. As already noted, everyone will want a piece of your time, and you need to be judicious in accepting meetings and activities. If the person responsible for scheduling is not provided with some explicit instructions, your schedule will not reflect your priorities and it will quickly fill up with meetings that lack purpose. Part of the meeting scheduling protocol should include duration and form. Rarely do one-on-one meetings require an hour, so consider using thirty minutes as the default duration. Also, where appropriate, substitute phone conversations or video conferencing for face-to-face meetings.

To build key relationships, a new executive leader should be proactive in scheduling visits with the key external stakeholders identified in the thirty-day plan. Prioritization is critical here. Many of these contacts will require travel, so you need to be strategic about who you visit. Further discussion of this activity is provided in chapter 8, "Managing External Relations."

Your time assessment should also include administrative policies and practices that govern the operations of the unit. While you should first try out the policies and practices that are already in place, you must be prepared to change them to fit your administrative style and priorities. Sometimes a fresh set of eyes is needed to identify practices that may no longer be serving the purpose that was once intended.

For example, signature approvals is an area in which I have noticed significant misallocation of time when entering a new position. Some organizations have developed a culture of requiring numerous signature authorizations to execute even the smallest of decisions. Obviously, you want to exhibit the appropriate amount of oversight of the unit's various functions, but it is not uncommon to find yourself signing documents and forms that pertain to areas about which you have no direct knowledge. When this occurs, it is appropriate to delegate these activities to people who are closer to the area of responsibility. This change can actually increase oversight and relieve you of frivolous paperwork.

When making these time prioritization decisions, a potentially helpful resource is your new primary administrative support person (administrative assistant, executive assistant, chief of staff). No one is more knowledgeable of the unit's day-to-day functioning and how your predecessor's time was allocated. This person will also likely have some good ideas about how to streamline processes and reallocate your time.

Speaking of executive assistants, there may be no other person who can have a greater impact on the success of an interim executive. As we all know, the right person can make your job much easier while the wrong one can lead to both parties being miserable daily. Your executive assistant can be an extraordinary resource to continue the normal day-to-day operations of the office, allowing you to focus on the right things. Most interim leaders spoke to the tremendous value of this person; however, a handful noted challenges in dealing with change-resistant administrative staff. An executive assistant who is not on board with you and your leadership can cause irreparable damage to your efforts.

Executive assistants who have worked with several interim leaders noted large differences in the smoothness of leadership transitions. The most significant issue identified was the level of independence they were afforded in conducting their jobs. Overmanaging staff members who had a high level of independence previously can stifle their effectiveness and decrease job satisfaction. This can work the other way, too. Giving autonomy to an assistant who was not afforded much independence by your predecessor can lead to challenges. It is useful to immediately sit down with the executive assistant and other key support staff—e.g., lead financial officer—and provide them with an opportunity to explain what, how, and why they do their job. Building mutual trust and respect with key support staff must be a top priority.

After a couple of months on the job, it could be useful to sit down with your executive assistant and complete an *ex post* look at your time allocation during month two. This analysis will reveal where you are spending your time (after the initial month of introductory activities) and allow you to make some quick adjustments.

Appropriate utilization of administrative staff can be overlooked by some executive leaders who assume interim positions, but these individuals can be great assets during a transition period.

Amanda, an interviewee who is an experienced executive assistant, worked with four different interim leaders. The first three all gave her significant latitude in completing normal office operations. She quickly gained the new leaders' trust and was able to continue to provide leadership in managing the day-to-day operations and deflect many policy- and process-related questions directed at the executive leader by employing her significant experience and knowledge of the position. Amanda continued to enjoy her job and felt she was contributing value to the institution by easing the transition of interim leaders.

The fourth interim leader restricted her independence, wanting to see and approve everyday operations, including those that were previously her responsibility. Amanda felt devalued and micromanaged. Her frustration was sufficient that she made her unhappiness known, and she was quickly hired away. As a result, the office lost a significant resource with unique first-hand knowledge of many operations, practices, and policies.

STAYING ON TASK

Structuring one's time is a continuing challenge in any administrative job. Leaders cannot do all the things that they would like to do or that others want them to do. Many who try end up plunging down a path to exhaustion and failure.

Administrators are surrounded by individuals and groups pressing them to give even more. This makes it easy to fill their days fighting fires and reacting to the endless stream of messages, meetings, calls, demands, and projects that come along. It's a seductive trap because it's an easy way to feel productive and needed. Administrators can get so busy they don't even notice that they've lost track of the big picture and have made little headway on the issues that really matter.

In coming into a new position, there is always a risk that new leaders will gravitate toward the parts of the job they enjoy and feel they're good at and ignore the parts of the job they dislike or aren't experienced at. It's like a right-handed person who favors their right arm—the muscles in the right arm will grow, but the muscles in the left arm won't. Try to become ambidextrous, so to speak, so that you are more well-rounded (Watkins 2013). The first step is to become aware of this possibility by identifying your strengths and weaknesses. The second step is to force yourself to prioritize job responsibilities in terms of importance rather than preference.

Covey's four-quadrant diagram of time management (Figure 4.1) is a useful typology for managing the numerous activities that face higher education executive leaders. While it may be a little dated, it still provides great guidance and a useful reminder of how to stay on task.

- **Quadrant I—Urgent and Important**
  The quadrant of necessities—here lie reactive tasks that need to be done, often at the last minute. Crises and looming deadlines are typical examples. This can be a challenge to manage, particularly during early

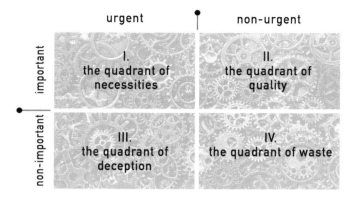

Figure 4.1. Covey's Four-quadrant Diagram of Time Management

periods of the interim appointment. There tend to be many alleged crises and a pent-up demand for decisions. Time spent in this quadrant can't be avoided, but it can be significantly reduced if you're focused on spending more time in Quadrant II.

- **Quadrant II—Important but Not Urgent**
  The quadrant of quality—these encompass proactive tasks, often habitual, that maintain or improve the quality of your work and life. Preparation, planning, and relationship building are typical examples. Strategic thinking about how to achieve the goals specified for the interim period is an important activity that falls in this quadrant. This is the quadrant you should aim to spend more time in. The more you expand this quadrant, the more you reduce the other three, particularly pseudo-emergencies that should never be allowed to become so.

- **Quadrant III—Urgent but Not Important**
  The quadrant of deception—most of us have encountered days when we have gone home in the evening wondering where all the time went—well, it was here. Many meetings and popular activities can be a poor use of your time, particularly when you are faced with the myriad of issues that are typically thrust upon interim leaders. This is the quadrant you are focusing on when restructuring your schedule as described above.

Again, carefully assess each of the regular meetings on the schedule. Take a hard look at meetings occurring within your unit and assess their usefulness. Consider meeting length and frequency. Can ninety-minute meetings be reduced to sixty minutes through improvements in organization and preparation? For many executives, the default appointment length is an hour; drop that back to thirty minutes and require that a longer meeting be justified. Become known for short, meaningful conversations.

Time management articles regularly cite unnecessary or lengthy conversations as some of the worst culprits of wasting time. This can be true, but the interim leader needs to be careful not to shorten the important conversations that establish relationships and put people at ease about the current changes.

- **Quadrant IV—Neither Urgent nor Important**
  The quadrant of waste—you know what it is, and you know when you've been in it. The trick is to know when you're in it and get out quickly. Busy work and some emails and phone calls fall into this category. Your administrative support staff can be critical allies in insulating you from this activity.

Finally, it is critical to know what is and what is not your business as an interim leader. There will be many people trying to command your attention and reaction to issues that are not within your scope of responsibility. These issues are by definition unimportant and fall into Quadrants III and IV. I have regularly had interim leaders in my own organization come to me with issues that are not their problem to solve. There are plenty of things to do without taking on issues others are charged with addressing. This problem again points to the importance of clearly defining roles and responsibilities up front.

Chapter 5

WORKING WITH YOUR NEW TEAM

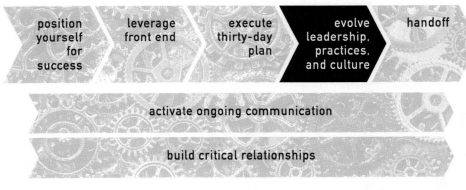

Figure 5.1. Interim Leadership Timeline, Stage 4: Evolve Leadership, Practices, and Culture

With any new administrative position comes a new team. There is little question that the success of any interim leader will be largely attributed to the work of this group. Team management is not always easy. Most of the time it means navigating different personalities, work habits, and motivations while balancing your own tasks and keeping the institution's goals top-of-mind.

Most interim executive leaders are not new to managing large, diverse teams, and have significant experience assessing, motivating, managing, and leading teams. Successful interim leadership involves deploying this skill set in the new and challenging environment. Interim leaders are unique in that they typically don't have the luxury of forming a team. They inherit a team from their predecessor, and with the exception of a few tweaks, that team is largely going to be in place throughout the interim period. That being the case, the task at hand is more about team shaping than team formation.

The secret of interim team management is to understand the people you will be working with so that you can make use of their strengths, motivations, and ways of doing business. As noted earlier, investing in relationships is a critical component of successful interim leadership. Leadership works when relationships work, and investing in these relationships may be the interim leader's most important early task.

Leadership transitions can be stressful to everyone within the organization but are particularly stressful to members of the leadership team. It is important to keep this reality in mind and focus on nurturing team members through the transition process. Some members of the team may feel marginalized or threatened. The goal is that everyone is valued, and seen as having value, so everyone is set up for success according to his or her skill, talent, role, and potential.

INITIAL ENGAGEMENT WITH THE TEAM

Initial engagement with a new team is critical to long-term success. Research conducted by Michael D. Watkins (2013) shows that what you do during the first thirty days of a job transition is what matters most. Your colleagues and your boss form opinions about you based on limited information, and those opinions are sticky. It's hard to change their minds, so it is important to shape their impressions to the best of your ability.

When you arrive on the job, and even beforehand, people will immediately begin to assess you and your capabilities. To some extent, these opinions will be based on what members of the team already know about you. Assume that people have done their homework on you by calling past colleagues to learn about you and your administrative style. Whether you like it or not, and whether it is deserved or not, you will bring a certain reputation into the new position. Be aware of this reputation and, to the extent that it is based on negative or untrue elements, work to change it. Research has shown that people often exhibit confirmation bias when encountering new colleagues or supervisors by focusing on information that confirms their beliefs and screen out information that does not.

When you assume responsibility for a new team, initial engagement should be a period rich in relationship building and collaboration. Resist the urge to needlessly assert your authority, and use questions to gain context regarding talent, operations, and opportunities. You need your team's help to succeed, and the right way to start out is by making your team members a valuable part of the process. In the beginning, it's good practice to observe and ask without judging.

Steps for advancing relationships with key members of the team should begin during the front end and continue through the interim's time of service. There is pressure for interims to deal with the immediate decisions and crises at hand and not invest adequately in relationships. This error can be avoided by being very intentional about relationship building and being a people-centered leader. Carve off time to invest in team building and individual relationship building activities. Identify the informal leaders and influencers within the team and make certain you are spending adequate time and effort building those relationships.

The priority goal in working with your new team is establishing mutual trust and respect (Zaniello 2019). The ongoing transition is a period of great stress for everyone. There is a lot of uncertainty, and people are worried about what the future may bring. It is critical that you communicate stability and confidence. Remember, they not only listen to what you say, they also watch what you do, so be very thoughtful about your interactions.

During this time, follow the adage, "Speak with confidence, lead with confidence." Self-confidence is the fundamental basis from which leadership grows. "Confidence equals security equals positive emotion equals better performance," says Tony Schwartz, president and CEO of The Energy Project and coauthor of *Be Excellent at Anything: The Four Keys to Transforming the Way We Work and Live*. People admire and like to work with leaders who are confident yet humble. There is a natural tendency to trust people more when they appear confident. For most of us, dealing with a confident person helps assure us that the person is also competent.

Communicating with confidence is a critical component of effective leadership. People don't want to follow leaders who show uncertainty and anxiety. Fear is contagious; so is confidence, but in a more productive direction. Critical to gaining credibility is our ability to be clear and crisp in our point of view while also being able to read different stakeholders and be responsive to their needs.

An immediate priority is to meet with the new leadership team. This important meeting should occur on the first day of your appointment, if not earlier. Make the meeting about them. Too often, new leaders step into a role and make a poor first impression by going on about their own background and experience. After a brief introduction, ask questions designed to help you better understand the leadership team's culture and working dynamics. Some possible questions to prime this discussion are:

- What are you proud of that this group does particularly well?
- What have been the major accomplishments over the last year?
- What are the current goals of the team?
- What is the biggest challenge you have overcome as a team?
- What are the most important opportunities on the horizon?

Keep the discussion positive and focused on team performance. Steer team members away from going off in a direction about their own or their unit's accomplishments.

The group meeting should quickly be followed by one-on-one meetings with members of the leadership team. These meetings allow you to continue developing key relationships and assess the leadership team through the perspective of each individual member. Again, you want to steer these conversations to the present and future, stay positive, and listen more than you speak. Some useful questions to consider for these meetings are:

- What are some of the most rewarding things about your job?
- What are some of the best/worst aspects of previous leaders you worked with?
- How would you like us to use our one-on-one time?
- What do you perceive to be some of the organization's key strengths, weaknesses, opportunities, and perils?
- What experiences at work make you stressed or frustrated?
- Do you have the resources and support to be successful?
- How would you like to receive constructive feedback?

Practice good listening skills during these meetings. Effective leaders are good listeners. When leaders first assume a position of responsibility, taking the time to hear and understand the people who make up the organization can help build rapport and credibility from the start. Gunsalus et al. (2019) identified three important reasons for emphasizing listening when taking on a new role: (1) listening shows respect and regard for the people you work with, (2) listening builds a broader sense of trust and community, and (3) listening broadens your perspective and helps you accumulate important information and reduce misunderstanding.

Also, avoid the temptation to talk about your previous position or organization too much. Nobody wants to hear or see that, especially if your old organization is perceived as a competitor. Certainly, you want to refer to past experiences to bring in new perspectives, but constant reference to your previous position can message that you are an outsider and living in the past as opposed to being focused on your new position in the present.

Successful team management involves more than engaging the leadership team. Everyone within the organization is a member of the team, and it is important to get in front of them as soon as possible. Schedule a large group meeting or, if necessary, a set of small meetings with the entire organization to introduce yourself, deliver your initial message, and reaffirm the timetable for finding a permanent successor. Keep the message simple and leave plenty of time for questions. The communication plan discussed in chapter 2 provides further guidance for engaging with this group throughout the interim period.

TAKING STOCK OF YOUR TEAM

Based on front end work, group meetings, one-on-one meetings, and initial observations, you can begin assessing team culture, behavior, and performance. Taking stock of the team really occurs at two levels—first, overall team functionality; second, the capabilities and performance of individuals comprising the team.

Assessing Team Culture and Performance

The success of any team is influenced by much more than the skills of the individuals comprising it. If skills were the only factor, the team with the highest payroll would win the World Series every year. The fact is, the team with the highest payroll (and by extension the best individual players) rarely wins championships. Assessing the new team requires a deep dive into the culture, behaviors, performance, working relationships and shared vision, commitment, and loyalty of the group. Once you have completed the first thirty days, it's time to reevaluate the BRAVE culture assessment referenced in chapter 1.

Some questions you might want to ask yourself in conducting your own assessment of the team follow:

- **How does this team fit with the organization's overall strategy and key goals?**
  Most things get done through the leadership team. If the team lacks the necessary skills and commitment, the interim leader will be thrust into a spiral of frustration and the organization will fail to move forward. The team was developed by a different leader for perhaps delivering on a different set of goals. Does the team have the ability to deliver on any new goals included in the action plan?

- **How dependent was the team's past performance on the personality and management of the outgoing leader?**
  Well-functioning teams are not leader-centric, but if you inherit one that is, additional work will be required to change the culture and allow them to spread their wings and fly, both individually and collectively.

- **What are the perceived strengths and weaknesses of the group?**
  New leaders should conduct a mini SWOT analysis of their team that is informed by drilling down on past performance, individual and group meetings, and observation of the team in action. For an experienced manager, these strengths and weaknesses tend to reveal themselves very quickly.

- **Does the group maximize available synergies?**
  Teams are assembled to bring diverse skills and perspectives to the table so that the total outcome is greater than the sum of the parts. Does the group function as a well-connected team or a loose confederation of individuals?

- **How does the team approach problem-solving?**
Does the group tackle problems by using a more collaborative and collegial approach or are problems addressed in a competitive and confrontational manner?

- **How deep is the talent on the team?**
Your assessment of individual team members will go a long way to answer this question. Are there any talent gaps that are limiting team performance?

- **Are there any flight risks within the leadership team?**
Leadership transition is often a time when people start looking for or considering other opportunities. Be on the lookout for these possibilities and try to assure key team members that they have a bright future in the organization.

- **How experienced is the team?**
Unfortunately, the escalation of position turnover across higher education reaches all levels of an organization, so it is likely that you may have some team members who have not been in place very long or are also interim leaders. These people will need more attention and mentoring.

The experience of team members in their respective positions can have a significant influence on the manner in which you lead the team as a whole and individual team members. It is important to carefully assess experience levels as quickly as possible.

When I began serving as interim president, the median tenure of the vice presidents and campus chancellors (some interim) was 2.6 years. Events prior to my appointment contributed to some departures within the leadership team and failures to replace them in a timely manner. The president was ill, and replacing departed administrators was justifiably not one of his top priorities. Two leadership positions were not even filled with interims when I stepped in. I immediately hired a couple of capable young leaders from within each unit to serve in interim roles. Two ongoing searches for executive leaders were continued, and we were able to successfully hire two excellent replacements, but those moves added to the overall lack of experience (at least as measured by time in their current position) across the leadership team. I did not fully realize the overall lack of experience across the leadership team until after I left the position and began to reflect on the previous year. It would have been useful to be more aware of the issue, and that insight would have certainly affected how I engaged with the leadership team. That oversight was on me.

Observe group dynamics in early meetings with the leadership team. Do you detect any alliances, coalitions, or conflicts? Are there informal leadership roles being exhibited? Who defers to whom on particular topics? Pay attention to nonverbal clues such as body language and facial expressions when specific issues are being discussed.

How do you tell if your team is really functioning well? You may instinctively sense that some element of teamwork is missing or that you can attain better performance if certain measures are taken. But rather than guessing, you should perform a structured team assessment to evaluate a team's strengths and weaknesses. There are numerous tools available for conducting team assessments. These tools differ in complexity from brief self-administered resources to consulting services involving significant face-to-face activities. For the interim leader, a straightforward self-administered assessment tool is probably appropriate. I would advise consulting with your human resources unit, as they may have tools available and can provide critical support in administration and interpretation. "Everything You Need to Know About Team Assessments" (Simon 2017) is an excellent summary of the how, what, when, and why of team assessments.

If you have inherited a dysfunctional organization, you need to be strategic about your messaging. Many members of the unit have been very loyal to the past leader and have worked hard, even if the outcomes were not optimal. You do not want to alienate or demoralize this group. Identify the issues without blaming past leadership and celebrate the achievements of the past. Engage with them about what worked well in the past and the accomplishments they are most proud of. Seek their constructive input on how their area within the organization can be improved and what support is needed.

If some members of the group are openly hostile about the change in leadership, it is important to clarify that you are not responsible for the decision to remove the previous administrator and you are there to assist them to move on in a positive direction. I once was asked to take on leadership of an organization after the president had deposed the previous leader. The first meeting with the team was a challenge, as the majority of the group was openly angry about the president's decision. Some even openly plotted about how they might overthrow the very powerful and highly respected president. I found it helpful to simply let the group vent without accepting any responsibility for the decision. After the venting process, it became obvious to all that our only recourse was to move on together. Patience with some of the most ardent loyalists was required to work through the grieving process.

Assessing Individual Team Members

While the new leader is ultimately concerned about team functioning and performance, there is a strong case to made that understanding individual team members is equally important to successful team management. Teams are comprised of individuals at different stages of their careers, each of whom has different skills, abilities, and aspirations. Individual assessment can be based on work done in the front end, your one-on-one meetings, and observing performance in the initial weeks of the interim appointment.

In assessing individual team members, often one of the first places you can start is forensically looking through paperwork. Are there performance reviews? Is there paperwork documenting performance issues and remediation steps? Are position descriptions up-to-date, and do they reflect each position's actual roles and responsibilities? Unfortunately, these materials are not always present, and oftentimes performance reviews can be pretty flimsy and provide little substantive information.

If you are being elevated from within the organization, you already have relationships with many members of the team. While these past relationships provide a head start in assessing team members, as a new leader you must remember that you are now operating in a completely different context. Making a sudden switch from peer to leader and supervisor is one of the most difficult challenges that some interims encounter.

Past interim leaders interviewed who were promoted from within the organization noted several different reactions, both positive and negative, from their former peers. Some former peers tried to pull them back to the previous relationship and maintain a peer-to-peer dynamic. This behavior must be immediately checked or it will be viewed as favoritism and compromise the leader's effectiveness. Others experienced a supportive community with the majority of team members going the extra mile to support the interim. In these cases, building a tight team culture without a strict hierarchy of authority is a useful approach.

Watkins (2013) proposes some insights for dealing with former peers when moving into a supervisory role:

- **Accept that the relationships must change.**
  An unfortunate reality of promotion within your unit is that personal friendships with former peers must become less so. Close personal relationships are rarely compatible with supervisory relationships.

- **Symbolism can be important.**
  Planning some symbolic gestures that emphasize your new role can be helpful in establishing that new role. For example, having your boss attend a meeting to pass the baton can affirm the new order.

- **Establish your authority deftly.**
  In this situation you must achieve the right balance between over- and under-asserting yourself. Err toward being overly consultative on critical issues until former peers get used to you making the calls.

- **Focus on what is good for the organization.**
  From the day you are appointed, some former peers will be vying for attention and favoritism. Adopt a relentless, principled focus on what is right for the organization.

If you are coming in from outside the organization, building individual relationships must be accomplished from the ground up. You are entering a situation where nearly everyone knows more about the local issues than you. Alliances and coalitions have already been formed, people have strong opinions about what should and shouldn't be done, and they all have plenty of evidence to support their views. You also have little knowledge of the culture and group dynamics of the organization. Those interviewed who were brought in from outside to lead a unit found this knowledge gap the most difficult to overcome. They also cautioned about imposing practices and processes from their former institution. Sometimes administrative responses that work in one setting do not fit another. On the other hand, "outsiders" noted that their previous experience provided credibility that they could leverage early in their tenure.

You will inevitably find yourself starting to form impressions of team members as you meet with them and observe them in group situations. It is important that you be conscious and intentional about the criteria you implicitly or explicitly use to evaluate people. Watkins (2013) proposes six criteria for assessing individuals on your team:

- **Competence**—does this person have the technical skills and experience to do the job effectively?

- **Judgment**—does this person exercise good judgment, especially under pressure, and make decisions for the common good of the organization?

- **Energy**—does this team member bring positive energy to do the job?

- **Focus**—is this person capable of setting priorities and sticking to them?

- **Relationships**—does this individual get along with others on the team and support collective decision-making, or is this person regarded as difficult to work with?

- **Trust**—can you trust this person to follow through on commitments?

The fundamental question to ask when assessing individual team members is whether you have confidence in them in the roles they are in or the ones the organization needs them to fill moving forward. Confidence is driven by the six criteria listed above, with one important addition—does the person have a track record of doing the job in a manner that is consistent with the culture and values you are trying to instill in the organization? Some of the most skilled, competent, and focused people can raise havoc in a team if they cannot execute in a manner consistent with team values.

As you assess individual team members, you should also be on the lookout for situations where individuals have not been supported by supervisors or fellow team members. Sometimes apparent underperformance may be the result of an employee being subjected to discriminatory treatment and/or microaggressions.

Another outcome of your individual assessments should be to identify your go-to people and those you might be able to access to deliver on priorities. Don't rely on the past leader's list as there are likely some unearthed gems who will shine under your leadership.

Based on your assessments, an individualized approach to engage each team member can be comprised of strategies such as more frequent check-ins, mentoring, skill development, reassignment, or largely leaving them alone to execute.

Responses of Team Members to an Interim Leader

People within an organization will respond differently to new leadership. For the most part, members of your new team will be very supportive and cooperative. They appreciate that you have stepped in to assist the organization and will do whatever is asked of them during the interim period.

While positive thinking may lead one to expect that everyone will respond to the interim leader in a positive manner, that is extremely naïve thinking. An organization of any size will likely have members who fall into one or more of the following categories:

- **Allies**

  These team players are clearly with you and have the health of the organization as their top priority.

- **Neutrals**

  The strategy of these individuals is to hunker down and keep their heads low to avoid any conflict. In some cases, this group constitutes the silent majority. This is an important group to gain favor with and turn into allies.

- **Detractors**

  Those comfortable with the status quo who are distrustful and suspicious of new leadership may perceive you as a threat to their values and/ or power or fear looking incompetent in a new system with different expectations. These people may have been in their positions for a long time, and they worry that there may be more to lose in giving up the current state than there is to gain in supporting change.

- **Snipers**
  While comprising a hopefully small or nonexistent cadre, these are disenfranchised team members who may be working behind your back to sabotage your leadership, sometimes because they feel they should have gotten the interim position. Typically, they have a track record of this behavior. It is important to find out who these people are from trusted members of your team. There are various ways of dealing with this situation, and it is best to first approach them in a positive and constructive manner. Don't ignore them.

- **Power-grabbers**
  These are people who use the absence of a permanent leader to try to gain additional power or work into areas where they were not permitted to operate under the previous leader. Remember Alexander Haig's infamous response following the 1981 assassination attempt on President Reagan: "I'm in control here." Such behavior can be unintentional or very intentional. Either way, these people need to be identified early and assertively managed.

Interim leaders have a short time window to correct poor team member behavior that causes distractions, dysfunction, and a losing culture. It is best to "nip this in the bud," redefining rules of engagement between team members and with the interim leader to create a winning culture.

When Patricia assumed the role of interim president, she immediately encountered two power-grabbers within her direct reports. Perhaps not surprisingly, from past interactions with the university administrative team when she was in the provost role, she had already identified them as individuals who might attempt to take advantage of the leadership transition. Patricia met with each person within the first month and explained her concerns about their behavior. Genuinely surprised with Patricia's proactive tactic, one was apparently motivated by a desire to pitch in and assist during a time of need. He immediately corrected his behavior. The other, who had unsuccessfully pursued greater independence with Patricia's predecessor, was not as willing to engage in self-reflection.

Despite collegial efforts to control the behavior, the independence-seeking executive continued to practice counterproductive behavior and was a distraction to the entire leadership team. Patricia was forced to set some firm ground rules for the remainder of the interim period, document them through written correspondence, and regularly monitor the situation. After the interim period, the incoming president quickly negotiated a path out of the institution for the unhappy executive.

Diversity, Equity, and Inclusion

In recent times, there has been an increasing imperative for colleges and universities to advance diversity and assure equity and inclusion for its students, faculty, and staff; however, the degree to which this agenda has inculcated various offices and academic units is varied. As noted in chapter 3, diversity, equity, and inclusion should be an important part of your thirty-day plan that can then drive your goals in this area for the remainder of the interim period. Perhaps your new unit has a leadership position—e.g., chief diversity officer, director of equity and diversity—who is providing capable leadership in this area. If so, your job is to empower this individual and communicate that this important work will continue during your leadership. If not, seek assistance from university-level resources that are available to provide assistance.

Diversity includes but is not limited to race, color, ethnicity, nationality, religion, socioeconomic status, veteran status, education, marital status, language, age, gender, gender expression, gender identity, sexual orientation, mental or physical ability, genetic information, and learning styles. One should resist the temptation to evaluate the diversity of the organization by observing team members. An important step in the onboarding process is a visit with the college or university's designated Office of Equal Opportunity (OEO) to discuss their perspectives on your new unit and any interactions, positive or negative, that they have been involved in recently. Also, to the extent that any data is available on the diversity of your unit, they will have it.

Recruiting a diverse team is an important first step, but assuring the workplace is equitable and inclusive is an even greater challenge. Equity concerns the guarantee of fair treatment, access, opportunity, and advancement for all members of the team while striving to identify and eliminate barriers that have prevented the full participation of some individuals and groups. Inclusion is authentically bringing traditionally excluded individuals and/or groups into processes, activities, and decision/policy-making in a way that shares power and ensures equal access to opportunities and resources.

When it comes to advancing diversity, equity, and inclusion in the workplace and in academic environments, the interim possesses some important advantages. First, the interim brings a fresh and unbiased perspective to the assessment of progress and needs in advancing these areas. Second, and most importantly, leadership matters, and when the new leader (even an interim) emphasizes the importance of diversity, equity, and inclusion, people will take notice. Finally, as noted before, impermanence has value. If systemic workplace climate problems are identified, a serious shake-up will be required. The interim can do this, and while all problems will not be corrected during the interim period, initiating the first steps to improving the workplace is a laudable outcome.

The disadvantage that the interim must overcome is a common one—a lack of knowledge and information about the culture of the organization and the seriousness with which issues of diversity, equity, and inclusion have been approached in the past. As I began one of my positions, it did not take long to identify that we had serious problems with gender discrimination and sexual harassment. Before my one-month anniversary, I had multiple visits from women faculty members asking that serious and repeated sexual harassment be addressed. Working with our OEO and campus attorneys, we were able to remove three offenders from the university within one year. People noticed. In my experience, it does not require a public pronouncement that you are going to be tough on violators. Word gets around very quickly, to both the victims and the harassers.

An expert panel commissioned by the Education Advisory Board recommends five actions to advance diversity, equity, and inclusion within your team:

- **Take responsibility.**
  Top administrators need to be directly involved in campus diversity issues and commit to the long run.

- **Include all faculty members in decisions.**
  Diversity plans tend to be hashed out by small groups of people with disproportionate minority representation and little power to enact

change on campus. "If faculty don't own an issue, it's impossible to make progress on it," says Brown University President Christina Paxson.

- **Bring students into the conversation.**
  College administrators can miss out on important conversations when they ignore, dismiss, or take at face value student demands that may come off as too extreme.

- **Call in the experts.**
  Conversations about campus diversity initiatives can be too complex for administrators to handle on their own. Sometimes it's best to invite diversity experts to assist.

- **Practice accountability.**
  If a diversity initiative fails, administrators need to recognize what went wrong and come up with new solutions. It's not okay to say, "We gave it a good try," and move on.

Allegations of discrimination are serious, and all colleges and universities have very specific policies on how they are to be handled. You should be well-versed on these policies prior to starting the interim appointment. In just about every case, an executive leader is a mandatory reporter, which requires you to report any allegation of discriminatory behavior. Perhaps the most frequent mistake of a new leader in handling discrimination complaints is to try to keep the issue within their own organization and deal with the accused employee oneself. Let the experts assist you in handling it.

What if the accusation of discrimination is directed at you? In this case, the best response is to self-report the allegation to OEO or the appropriate unit for handling discrimination complaints. This approach will assure that the complainant receives a fair treatment of the allegation. It also allows you to avoid any criticism that you are trying to cover up the issue or address it with people who are under your span of supervision.

ADDITIONAL STRATEGIES FOR ENGAGING THE TEAM

The best gift an interim leader can give to the successor is a well-functioning team. If you inherit a team that shares a common vision, culture, and set of values; behaves in a collegial and synergistic manner; and performs at a high level, your task is more about shaping and might focus more on coaching individual team members. If you have a team that is not functioning well, the rebuild needs to start with values and culture. Until the team starts operating under a common set of values and goals, with a focus on advancing the entire organization—as opposed to each individual unit's welfare—team performance will not improve.

Being promoted to an interim leadership role from within the unit can present some unique challenges, particularly if significant behavioral change within the unit is required. The interim leader must make a clear break from past peer-to-peer relationships and establish leader-to-peer relationships.

Tim, an interim dean, was promoted from within his college. Suddenly, he was thrust into the role of leading his former peers to address some extremely difficult personnel and fiscal challenges. He definitely had taken on the role of a "clean up the mess" interim leader. During the tenure of the previous two deans, the college had developed a culture where academic units acted independently and with little oversight or accountability to the dean's office. Not surprisingly, this culture had resulted in inconsistent performance across units and large financial overruns, and the college had routinely underachieved in meeting its performance metrics. The leadership team lacked a shared vision and commitment to the college, and leaders acted as individual agents trying to maximize the resources being allocated to their own units.

The provost saw this dysfunction and selected an interim leader who understood the problem and possessed the necessary leadership skills to begin the process of building a more accountable organization. Tim immediately received pushback from several of his former peers who did not see the problem. They tried to convince him to cut them special deals, citing their past relationships as justification for being treated as an exception. Tim held several two- to three-hour leadership meetings focused on defining the problems facing the college, building team solutions, and implementing various accountability measures. A couple of unit leaders resigned because they did not like the new direction, and Tim replaced them with people who embraced the new challenge. Those replacements were "game changers," and from that point on, the team's group functioning was dramatically improved. The interim period resulted in several substantive improvements that positioned the college in a much better place for the incoming permanent dean.

Be prepared for the onslaught. One of the most important reasons to meet with the team early is to control the inevitable onslaught of meeting requests that will come immediately upon your arrival. Many within the organization will feel compelled to contact you for what they term urgent meetings. Unfortunately, their definition of urgent might not align with yours. Trying to accommodate all these requests is a way to spend an inordinate amount of time on urgent, unimportant (Quadrant III) activities.

The interim leader need not accept all past determinations as set in stone. While it is unnecessary to assess all recent decisions, new leaders must sometimes be prepared to revisit past determinations and perhaps say no to decisions that were previously given the green light. Trying to honor all past commitments (unless there is a legal obligation) can sometimes be counterproductive for the organization.

Another challenge many interim leaders experience is sorting out the numerous alleged deals that were made with the predecessor. As one might expect, these "deals" may or may not reflect an actual agreement with the previous leader. The predecessor, if accessible, can be helpful in providing perspective on the situation.

As noted earlier, impermanence has value. That holds true in personnel management as well. Interim leaders are perceived differently from permanent leaders. Their temporary status and neutrality can be used to establish open and candid lines of communication with members of the team. This can have both favorable and unfavorable consequences. People often take the opportunity of new leadership to reengage, but be aware of people who want to revisit past grievances and effect a different outcome.

A challenge sometimes faced by interim leaders is how to handle commitments made by their predecessor. Obviously, if they are contractual in nature—e.g., a salary increase included in an offer letter—they will need to be honored. However, many commitments are informal and may need to be revisited if they don't support the new direction of the unit.

An interim president, Phyllis followed a president who had passed away while in office and was known to engage in making verbal agreements. She was immediately besieged with requests to confirm and adhere to what some viewed as past commitments. These requests ranged from waiving the tuition of an employee's child to constructing a new building for an academic program. For most of these alleged commitments, there was no written record, and no one within the office of the president or the vice president for finance had any recollection of the offer.

Phyllis implemented a policy that only written commitments would be honored, and others would need to be reevaluated on a case-by-case basis. Even written commitments would only be honored if they conformed with state and university policies and passed what Phyllis referred to as the "headline test." Several people were very upset about what they viewed as a failure of the university administration to make good on its commitments; however, they could not produce written corroboration of the commitment or an objective third party who was privy to the commitment.

Invariably, when coming into a new executive position, you will discover past decisions or commitments that leave you scratching your head. What might have been rational a year or two ago may not make sense today. Addressing these "gifts that keep on giving" is one of the great services interim leaders can provide their successor.

Team Management Pitfalls

Just as there are critical strategies for managing your new team, there are certain behaviors to avoid at all costs. In *Leadership Land Mines: Eight Management Catastrophes and How to Avoid Them* (2005), Marty Clarke provides an excellent summary of some of these behaviors. We have all seen these leadership missteps in practice, and it is useful to keep them in mind as you go about the process of working with a new team.

1. It's All about Me

This situation rears its ugly head anytime a manager's decisions and actions are not ruled by the needs of the organization but by their own agenda or desire for personal gain. There is no quicker way to lose the trust of a new team than to operate in this manner.

2. The Popularity Priority

When leaders make decisions based on what is most popular rather than what is best for the organization, their credibility is quickly compromised. Interims can fall into this trap because they are trying to gain favor with their team members.

3. The Super Doer

This scenario occurs anytime leaders identify a problem or issue that should be handled by a team member but instead jump in and resolve the issue themselves. Obviously, this is not a practice that will instill confidence in team members.

4. The Blame Addiction

This occurs when managers spot a problem and then, instead of fixing it, spend valuable time and energy trying to assign blame. Interims need to be particularly careful not to exhibit this behavior with a problematic situation inherited from the predecessor. Consciously avoiding the blame game will focus the team on solutions and prevent defensive reactions of team members who may have contributed to the current situation.

Mark was appointed interim dean of a large college following his recent retirement from a deanship at another university. The college was experiencing financial duress, and Mark was brought in by his former colleague, now the provost, to provide an outsider's perspective and "get the college to a state where someone would want to take the permanent job." After a couple of introductory meetings with his leadership team, Mark approached the fiscal situation head-on by presenting a summary of the college's present financial condition and a summary of past annual fiscal performance. Many members of the leadership team quickly went into "blame game" mode, citing their colleagues' poor management of their academic units. While Mark did not identify specific units or managers, he quickly reminded the team that this was a college-wide problem and as the college leadership team, they all were responsible for addressing the issue.

Mark followed up with each member of the leadership team to review their unit's own fiscal situation, which served as a reminder to some of the "blamers" that they were contributors to the problem. He had significant credibility because of his lengthy experience and the clear direction from the provost. Over the next year, the team worked together to develop policies and processes to begin whittling away at the budget deficit and hold each other accountable as members of the leadership team. The new environment was a critical factor in enabling the college to hire a capable permanent dean from an aspirational university.

5. Managing to the Exception

This condition arises when a leader allows an idea to be shot down because it's not perfect or when small consequences dictate decisions in matters of large consequences. As the old saying goes, "Perfection is the enemy of progress," and seeking the perfect plan is a certain way to assure the status quo.

6. Cloudy Expectations

When a leader initiates a project or activity without setting clear expectations for the people participating or for the project itself, the project can stagnate or never come to fruition. New leaders need to guard against this pitfall and correct any inherited projects lacking clear expectations.

7. Confrontation Phobia

When new leaders choose not to confront an issue because it's easier to take the path of least resistance, they are likely to quickly lose the respect and confidence of their team. This behavior is particularly baneful when applied to personnel management. Failure to take on poorly behaving personnel will empower the individual(s) and disappoint other team members waiting for relief.

8. Managing by Committee

This form of administrative paralysis occurs anytime progress slows or a critical decision is delayed because group consensus is required.

Unfortunately, this scenario often occurs in higher education leadership where there is an environment of collaborative decision-making. Obviously, collaboration is a positive thing, but consensus can be elusive when it comes to making difficult decisions, and it is ultimately up to the leader to decide and assume accountability.

Addressing a Toxic Work Environment

When conducting your team assessment, you should be on the lookout for signs of a toxic work environment. Toxic cultures take over a workplace when the interactions between employees or between supervisors and employees become so negative that they no longer meet socially acceptable norms for civility. Employees in toxic workplaces show less engagement with work and feel devalued, unappreciated, bullied, maybe even harassed. Some common signs of a toxic work environment are poor individual or team performance, high employee turnover, team members afraid to voice their opinions, leadership tolerant of offensive statements about coworkers and other inappropriate behavior, and leaders who blame team members and don't hold themselves accountable.

In the rare event that you inherit an organization with a toxic work environment, it is imperative that the situation be identified and addressed quickly. Leadership is the only antidote for a toxic work environment, and the introduction of a new leader can be the structural break needed to move the organization in a positive direction.

Some strategies to consider in addressing the situation are:

- **Reinforce the notion of a team.**
  It is essential to include employees when you set out to establish a workplace where their safety and wellbeing are priorities. The task of company leaders is to reengage employees and convince them that their lives will be better.

- **Neutralize the toxic behavior.**
  You need to stop the bad behavior before you can address the larger issues that left it unchecked. If you spot the problems early enough, you may be able to change the employee's behavior by establishing clear boundaries and calling out the offending behavior. Document the behavior that is raising your concerns. This will help you keep track

of progress, and it will also be a useful written record if disciplinary action is required.

- **Consider bringing in a third party.**
Acknowledging that the workplace has become toxic is an important step for the organization. Tracking the cause presents more difficulties, especially if workers are reluctant to come forward to report negative experiences. A third party is often able to identify the behaviors and attitudes that are having a detrimental effect on morale more effectively than managers, and employees are more comfortable sharing information with someone not entrenched in the company.

- **Look for the toxic worker.**
Finding the immediate source of the problem is paramount and can lead to a single individual. The toxic worker is not just unsuited to the position or an underperformer; he or she is harmful to the organization itself and can have an outsized effect on the workplace. The worker can set off a contagion in the office, whether fellow employees emulate the behavior, fall victim to it, or become so demoralized that they leave the company.

HIRING PERSONNEL AS AN INTERIM LEADER

One of the greatest personnel dilemmas for an interim is to decide whether to hire positions that come open or leave them open to be hired by the permanent successor. Obviously, positions reporting to lower level permanent leaders should continue to be hired. You don't want to create a cascading effect of interim leaders. I have seen cases where the failure to hire during the tenure of an interim executive leader created a unit paralyzed by the presence of interim appointments throughout the organization. As a result, the job of the incoming permanent leader became even more difficult and the return to normalcy was protracted.

For direct reports, the decision is more complicated. There are several key criteria to consider when deciding whether to go forward with replacing a position or waiting for the permanent leader to arrive. Among these are: (1) the expected duration of the interim leader's tenure, (2) the availability of a competent and qualified interim, (3) the position's importance to mission and delivery, and (4) the importance of the relationship with the executive leader to the position's success.

Two university president interviewees who preceded their permanent appointments with a year of interim service explained some rationale for delaying hiring. Provost, athletic director, and vice president for development were examples of positions they identified as best for the interim to avoid hiring. The provost is critical to the success of a president, and most presidents want to hire their own person into this position. As most presidents of universities with major athletic programs will tell you, the athletic director position is one that requires close monitoring, and presidents want to make certain they have the right person in place. Vice presidents of development work very closely with presidents, and the right fit for this position can be very dependent upon personality.

Hiring members of your team can be challenging as an interim leader. People generally like to know who they are going to work for; but I was successful hiring some very good vice presidents as an interim president and, likewise, deans as an interim provost. Previous interim presidents and provosts interviewed noted similar success. One useful strategy is to involve the next level up in the interviews. For example, if hiring a dean as an interim provost, the president can be helpful in meeting candidates and providing some certainty. Also, emphasize the strength of the organization and reduce the emphasis on you as the supervisor. Communicating a clear sense of purpose and strategy can reduce the anxiety that dramatic changes might occur with the hiring of the permanent leader.

Remember, one of your primary goals is to set up the incoming executive for success. A means of doing this is to initiate a new search and time it such that the incoming leader can participate in interviews and make the selection. This strategy can be very helpful for a new leader seeking to jump-start his or her own first one hundred days.

Chapter 6

DECISION-MAKING AND CHANGE MANAGEMENT

Leaders are expected to make things better and move the organization forward in a rapidly changing higher education environment. Interim leaders are no exception; in fact, often they are asked to assess and implement change at a much faster rate than someone assuming a permanent role. Based on assessment activities during the front end and first thirty days, priority areas or issues are identified to address in the action plan. How does the interim leader go about moving forward with the necessary changes?

LEAD WITH A BIAS TOWARD ACTION

In their classic business book and *New York Times* bestseller *In Search of Excellence* (2006), Thomas Peters and Robert Waterman scoured America's businesses and identified forty-three top performers. They then intensely studied these firms for two years to identify their commonalities. The first common principle identified was a bias for action—extraordinary companies are 100 percent focused on getting things done, and, by extension, so are their leaders. In many larger (and not so effective) companies, people spend a lot of time in meetings debating why things can't get done. What is needed in the workplace is a mindset where people's primary focus is on delivering results.

Implementing a culture focused on action can be particularly challenging in higher education. People who self-select into the profession tend to be risk-averse, and faculty are trained to question and debate propositions. Decision-making often requires considerable analysis and effort to develop consensus. This challenge is even more daunting for interim leaders, given the expectation that they may be stepping out of the role in a year or less.

Nonetheless, few interim leaders are appointed to preserve the status quo. The supervisor and team members within the organization will likely expect the interim leader to accomplish certain things, as will the interim leader themselves. Most interim leaders interviewed came to their position with an optimistic and aggressive set of goals to achieve during their appointment. They also noted that this paradox between their personal bias for action and the organization's grip on the status quo can be one of the greatest challenges to navigate.

Former interim executives identified several areas they found most critical to act on during their time in the position. First and foremost were the goals assigned by the supervisor, typically areas prioritized as important to address before a permanent leader came on board. Second were areas they identified as necessary to address due to their internal assessment during the first few months on the job. Third were ongoing projects and activities inherited from the previous administration that required completion in a timely manner. Keeping focused on these goals identified in the post-thirty-day action plan will deliver meaningful outcomes.

FRAMING SITUATIONS CORRECTLY

From an outside view, it appears that effective leaders have an uncanny ability to read situations quickly and accurately. This is a powerful skill given the volume of decisions that university administrators are faced with daily. This skill is not an inherited talent; it comes from practice and experience.

A challenge for interim leaders is that the experiential base specific to the position and some of the situations they may encounter are often not present when they begin their appointment. The transferability of their own experiences to the current position can differ significantly by situation. There is an inherent risk in employing previous framing mechanisms to the new situation, as they may not be quite right and lead to poor decision-making.

In my own situations, I found that most of my previous experience as a department head was transferable when I stepped into the role of dean. Similarly, my experience as a dean was highly transferable to the role of interim provost. The provost is principally focused on academic program administration and faculty affairs, which is common to both dean and academic unit leadership. Hence, it was relatively easy to move from one side of the table to the other. Moving from provost to interim president was a completely different experience. While there were several areas where I was working in close collaboration with the president, there were other administrative areas that I experienced for the first time—e.g., intercollegiate athletics, long-term capital financing, Greek life, and "town and gown" relations.

How, then, should an interim respond? Paradoxically, making deep, quick, and accurate situational analyses often requires one to slow down. When you are feeling overwhelmed by everything coming at you, slowing down is counterintuitive; however, it can be helpful in assuring that you are viewing situations accurately and from different perspectives.

Actively and regularly solicit input from others. This strategy allows you to look at a situation from a variety of perspectives and reframe. Ask for feedback. People are uncertain whether, as a leader who is new to the organization, you want input or tend to hole up. Asking is the easiest way to encourage them to provide feedback and input into decisions. Refer back to the learning plan in your thirty-day plan to be sure you are addressing knowledge gaps that occur during your service as interim.

A former colleague used to preach the "notice, adjust, and evolve" approach, which is a useful framework in these situations. You are not going to get everything right the first time. When the world does not quite make sense and our actions are producing the wrong results, it is time to reframe, look at the situation from different perspectives, and evolve your approach.

MANAGING CHANGE

Much has been written about change management in organizations. Most organizations today are in a constant state of flux as they respond to the fast-moving external business environment, local and global economies, and technological advancement. This means that workplace processes, systems, and strategies must continuously change and evolve for an organization to remain competitive. This phenomenon can be an uncomfortable reality within higher education.

Change management in higher education is particularly challenging because of the loose organizational structures that typically characterize colleges and universities. Other structural elements present in higher education institutions—such as tenure, shared governance, and academic freedom—can also complicate the execution of critical change initiatives.

Most of the successful colleges and universities of today are dynamic organizations that are nimble in their response to opportunities and don't operate under the timelines of yesteryear. These institutions are typically first-to-market with new programs in response to external forces such as technological change. They have also been highly responsive in deploying their human capital and other assets to nontraditional enterprises that create new revenue streams. Leaders in these institutions have figured out how to operate quickly and efficiently within the university environment while still respecting their academic institution's norms and values. Some organizations within institutions—e.g., academic colleges—have also set themselves apart as nimble and responsive.

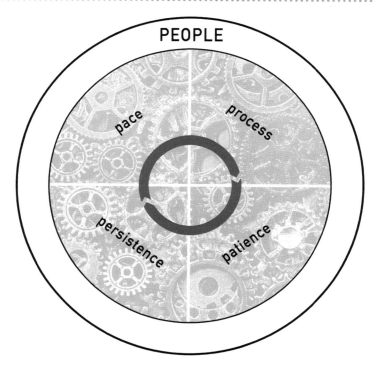

Figure 6.1. The Five P's of Effective Change Management

What are the keys to effective change management? Executing change within higher education institutions involves five P's: first and foremost, people, followed by process, pace, patience, and persistence.

Change affects your most important asset—people. Change should be considered and executed while maintaining your human capital as a top priority. Change affects people differently. For some, change is invigorating and stimulates excitement and creativity. For others, it can create anxiety, even to the point where they may elect to leave the organization.

In his book *Managing Transitions*, change strategist William Bridges documents a three-phase psychological process that people go through when encountering change. The first phase, "ending," involves the person letting go of their old perspective. Next, the "neutral phase" is a sort of "no man's land" in between the old reality and what the future holds. Finally, the "new beginning" involves starting over again with new passion, vision, and a sense of purpose.

Not only is change a process of transition with stages, it is also a process that will be approached differently by different people. The length of time team members spend in each of these phases will differ, depending upon a variety of factors, including their behavior style, the nature of the change and its impact on their daily lives, and the work environment and culture. Fortunately, their movement through these phases is also influenced by management's guidance. Within a team, there will be a range of behavioral styles, and each person will require a different approach to coach them through the transition.

A key to bringing people along is to recognize the existing norms of legitimate process. Process is essential to assess and adhere to expectations of how things should be done, and these processes often define the pace of change. An interim leader must be keenly aware of the culture of the organization related to change and thoughtfully develop a plan for implementing change. Patience can be vital because the wheels of change rarely move very fast in colleges and universities. Many university administrators, including myself, have learned the hard way that practicing patience is sometimes the fastest way to get to the desired outcome. A sure way to stymie progress is to move too fast and be forced to backtrack in order to relieve anxiety and address resistance to change.

Persistence is the vital ally of patience. Carrying through processes to fruition often requires an unwavering commitment to accomplishing the end goal.

A change management plan can support a smooth transition and ensure employees are guided through the change journey. The plan should be rooted in thorough communication and a pace that brings everyone along, and it should be embedded in accepted processes.

Steps for Effective Change Management

Seven essential steps to effective change management are illustrated in Figure 6.2. These are useful to review prior to initiating a significant change.

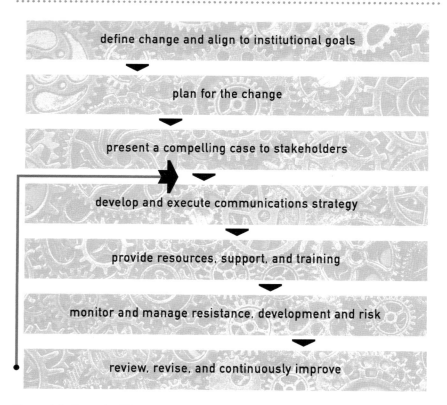

define change and align to institutional goals

plan for the change

present a compelling case to stakeholders

develop and execute communications strategy

provide resources, support, and training

monitor and manage resistance, development and risk

review, revise, and continuously improve

Figure 6.2. Steps for Effective Change Management

1. Clearly define the change and align it to institutional goals.

Since most change occurs to improve a process, program, or outcome, it is critical to identify the focus and clarify goals. It might seem obvious, but many ineffective change processes miss this first vital step. This step can also assist you in determining the value of the change, which will quantify the effort and inputs you should invest. Focus and clarification also involve identifying the resources and individuals needed to facilitate the process and lead the endeavor. Most change systems acknowledge that knowing what to improve creates a solid foundation for clarity, ease, and successful implementation. Aligning the change to institutional values and goals and articulating this conformation to the team is a critical step in legitimizing the proposed change.

2. Plan for the change.

Once you know exactly what you wish to achieve and why, determine the impacts of the change across the organization. Review the effect on each unit and how it cascades through the organizational structure to the individual. A roadmap should be developed that identifies the starting point, route to be taken, milestones, and destination. A critical element of planning is providing a multistep process rather than sudden, unplanned, sweeping changes.

3. Present a compelling case to stakeholders.

As noted above, buy-in is critical and requires a compelling case for why the change is necessary. There are several layers of stakeholders who likely need to be consulted, including the leadership team, upper management, affected parties, and those who are directly charged with implementing the "new normal." Make certain that the outcome is emphasized in making your case; change is uncomfortable for most people, so they need to clearly see the benefits of engaging in the change process.

It is this step that can be most challenging for interim leaders. In this case, impermanence does not have value, and people will often resist change with the rationale that the new permanent leader may not agree with the change.

4. Plan and implement a communication strategy.

The first three steps will have highlighted those employees to whom you absolutely must communicate the change. Determine the most effective means of communication needed to bring the group or individual on board. The communication strategy should include a timeline for how the change will be incrementally communicated as well as key messages and the communication channels and mediums you plan to use. Don't forget to celebrate success along the way. Recognizing milestone achievements and the efforts of teams and individuals involved is an important element of successful change management.

5. **Provide resources, support, and training.**
As part of the planning process, resource identification and funding are crucial elements. These can include items such as infrastructure, personnel, equipment, and software systems. Within higher education, change processes are often initiated without adequate resources. People are wary of these situations and their impact on the organization as well as their personal job satisfaction. So, it is important to adequately resource the change process and articulate the resources being allocated to assure success. Pay particular attention to how the change may affect people. Providing support and training for people whose daily lives will be impacted by the change will assist in reducing anxiety and resistance.

6. **Monitor and manage resistance, dependencies, and risks.**
Resistance is a very normal part of change management, but it can threaten the success of a project. Anticipating and preparing for resistance by arming leadership with tools to manage it will aid in a smooth change life cycle. Continuous communication is the most important tool for mitigating resistance.

7. **Review, revise, and continuously improve.**
As much as change is difficult and even painful, it is also an ongoing process. Review of progress, measurement, and monitoring should be woven through all steps. Measures and data for monitoring progress should be included in the change management plan developed in step 2 above. Changes to this plan will be necessary as the project evolves.

Change Management Considerations for the Interim

What is different about change management for the interim? First, the time frame that interim leaders often confront can be challenging. Change processes can take time and may require more time than the interim plans to be in the position. Second, the power dynamics are different for an interim than a permanent leader, and it is often alleged that they lack the power to implement change. The third and perhaps most significant distinction is the impermanence factor—i.e., convincing the team and others affected by the change that, despite the interim's limited tenure, the proposed change will remain in place into the future.

If time is really pressing, change agents may face a classic administrative dilemma: is it better to be on a fast train that might jump the track or a slow one that may arrive too late to be useful? Again, impermanence can have value. There are changes an interim can make that are potentially highly difficult for an incoming permanent leader. It is important for the interim leader to look for these opportunities.

Sometimes, it is not necessary to complete the entire change management process for the interim leader to be successful. Interim leaders have a unique opportunity to "set the table" for their successor by launching needed initiatives that can provide the incoming leader with a head start in addressing a key issue. Similarly, interims can assist the successor by taking on changes that may generate political repercussions.

It is often the case that an interim leader inherits an organization with long-term issues that have not been addressed because of the political fallout that might result from taking them on. An interim leader can be just the person to take on these challenges and make much-needed change, thus taking the administrative burden off an incoming administrator.

One interim dean, Carla, inherited a college with some very poor-quality space, including the college's administrative headquarters. The lone exception was a beautifully renovated building across the street that housed one of the college's academic units. Carla took the opportunity to move the college headquarters into one floor of the renovated building, which provided a more attractive and professional location. She first made the case to the college leadership team and then worked with her team to find suitable space for displaced faculty and staff. Resources were allocated and minor renovations completed to lessen the disappointment of affected parties. Of course, the displaced faculty and staff were not happy, but as interim dean, Carla was able to take the hit for the long-term betterment of the college.

Renovating administrative space can be a third-rail project for a new dean; Carla was able to tackle this politically charged issue and protect her successor. The change also signaled that she was willing to take on tough issues and the interim period was not going to be one dedicated to maintaining the status quo.

An absence of power is often cited as a significant impediment to the interim leader's ability to effect long-term change. The thinking is that the projected short duration of the position limits the interim's ability to influence people, build winning coalitions, and advance initiatives. This is not always the case, as politically astute interim leaders still have ample opportunities to engage in successful change management. At times, the position's temporary nature can even be a strategic advantage in effecting change, as in the previous case.

Power is a complex and fluid phenomenon that is often misunderstood. In many people's minds, power carries a negative connotation—something that bad people use to ride roughshod over good people. Power is simply the capacity to influence, to make things happen. Power is not derived simply from long-term supervisory responsibility or authority; it can also be gained through effective navigation of the political environment.

Colleges and universities are highly political institutions; that is a statement of fact, not an indictment. "Politics" is an overused and abused term. It is true that academic leaders must advocate, negotiate, bargain, compromise, build coalitions, and manage conflict to advance their agendas. If that is one's definition of politics, then politics is certainly a reality of higher education leadership. The challenge for campus leadership is to understand and leverage the political realities that are present in various situations.

The disadvantage interim leaders face is that even if they are from the same institution, they may not be familiar with power dynamics of the new position. Similarly, they often do not have networks and coalitions built to advance their agendas. Nonetheless, for the right initiatives, coalitions can be built and buy-in achieved with a compelling rationale, adhering to the five P's, and following the steps of effective change management.

An important step for the interim leader is to convince people that the changes being implemented will not be reversed when the permanent leader is in place. The best way to overcome that resistance is to make such a compelling case for the change that most members of the team can see its value. Obviously, that can be easier said than done, but the best way to reach people is to demonstrate that the change will actually make their life easier. Focusing your efforts on convincing formal and informal leaders of the proposed change's positive elements will also pay dividends. Ideally, they have been integral players in developing the change proposal and are thus already allies.

Gaining the endorsement of a proposed change from upper management is certainly another effective means to convince people of a change's permanency. Similarly, it is easier to gain buy-in for changes associated with delivering on directives stipulated by the president or provost for the interim period.

Interim leaders from outside the organization can possess an advantage in taking on issues that might be politically charged. The fact that the interim leader does not have any personal history with the issue and has not been part of past debates can be a strategic advantage in navigating conflict.

Drew, an interim provost, was recruited from outside the institution by the new president. Since several deans were potentially interested in the provost position, the president did not want to signal any preference prior to the search. She therefore chose to go outside the institution to fill the interim role. The interim provost was a colleague of the president at a previous institution, and she had confidence in his abilities to lead the academic enterprise while a new provost was being sought. Knowing Drew's passion and knowledge around issues of campus climate, equity, and diversity, the president asked him to initiate an equity and diversity initiative during the interim period. Drew launched the initiative at the beginning of a period of nationwide campus unrest around equity and diversity issues and provided his successor with a leg up in proactively addressing this critical issue on their campus.

The president also asked Drew to work with the deans and faculty senate to modernize the process required for academic program reviews and approvals of new programs. Given the circumstances—Drew did not have much knowledge of power dynamics within the institution—the fact that he had the backing of the new president was more than adequate to gain cooperation. Following established processes, he was able to hand off a near-complete policy for program review and approval.

GETTING STRUCTURE RIGHT

Keep in mind that you have not only inherited a team but also a structure and a set of roles that may range from either tightly defined or loosely implied. Don't assume that the structure and roles are properly defined. Part of your job during the front end and the first thirty days is to make this assessment.

As Jim Collins (2001) so plainly states, "You need to get the right people on the bus and in the right seats." Depending upon the functionality of the office, you may need to spend some time clarifying the position descriptions of team members and agreeing on their various roles and responsibilities. If you were able to review position descriptions during the front end, you can use these to structure your initial conversations with team members. While this activity could take more time than you would like to allocate, gaining clarity in roles and expectations will serve you well for the remainder of your tenure in the position.

It can be surprising and troubling to encounter past administrative neglect when assuming an interim position. If this occurs, correcting the situation by instilling the appropriate policies, procedures, and practices can provide a better starting point for your successor.

Jack, a former interim president, inherited a situation where there were no current position descriptions for the direct reports. When he requested performance reviews for team members, he found out that performance reviews had not been conducted in the previous five years. While the team was somewhat functional, not surprisingly, he discovered considerable role ambiguity, and members of the team were unfamiliar with much of their colleagues' work. Sometimes team members clashed over overlapping areas of responsibility.

Over the twelve months of Jack's interim leadership, all position descriptions were updated and performance reviews were conducted for all team members. Because the performance reviews were completed without any prior reviews to reference, they were largely forward-looking and addressed each team member's anticipated outcomes for the coming year. This work provided a tremendous head start for the incoming president when it came to assessing the roles and responsibilities of various members of the leadership team as well as their performance in these positions.

Studying the organizational structure of higher education institutions and the administrative units that comprise them—e.g., vice presidential areas, academic colleges, provost's and president's offices—can be perplexing at best. Some of the most convoluted organizational structures, which violate even the most basic tenets of organizational theory, are present in colleges and universities. Oftentimes, they reflect the personality and administrative style of the previous leader and can be reflective of years of organizational decisions that might have made complete sense at the time but today translate to inefficiency at best and sometimes dysfunction.

Educational institutions are known to be notoriously flat and loosely coupled, in the sense that linkage among organizational units may be infrequent, weak, or circumscribed (Bolman and Gallos 2011). Structure should (1) maximize support and minimize barriers to the work that needs to be done, (2) pull things together efficiently and effectively, and (3) facilitate good communications across the organization. When it doesn't accomplish these ends—or worse, when it creates stalemate in executing change—it needs to be reordered.

One of the quandaries faced by interim leaders is whether to change the inherited administrative structure. New leaders, including interims, often inherit organizations that are not structured correctly or at least in a manner that enables them to operate effectively. While the structure may have been appropriate for the previous leader, that might not be the case for someone new to the role. In addition, the structure may have been a primary source of the challenges encountered if the predecessor's departure was fueled by ineffectiveness. Again, your job is to set up the new permanent leader; so, if you encounter these structural issues, you may need to address them.

Significant organizational restructuring is normally not within the purview of the interim leader; however, it is necessary to have an administrative structure that is at least functional during the transition period. Several options exist that can improve functionality without tackling a full-scale restructuring.

When I assumed the role of interim president, I was perplexed by the number of direct reports. By the time we completed our inventory, we determined that the president had no fewer than thirty-two direct reports. While my experienced predecessor preferred a flat organization and seemed to manage it ably, it quickly became clear to me that something had to change. While vice presidents and campus chancellors as direct reports made sense, the list also included assistant vice presidents, administrative staff, communications professionals, budget staff, and a dean. While we can debate how many direct reports is optimal, there is no management text that would advocate for a number larger than thirty. It was clear that many of these people were not being adequately supervised, and I knew that I did not have the time to do it. By the end of the third week, I had the number of direct reports down to seventeen. Certainly, not everyone was happy because people like the prestige of reporting to the president and the ones not being supervised enjoyed their independence; but when the restructuring was complete, we had a much more manageable and accountable organization moving forward.

Many problems administrators face call for structural responses, and the interim leader cannot be afraid to respond. Restructuring can be highly disruptive, so it needs to be carefully thought through and the benefits and costs accurately assessed. Restructuring is an important option to consider when one encounters the final two scenarios of the typology presented in chapter 3:

- **Converge and Evolve Quickly**—when your analysis indicates that significant changes are required immediately to deliver expected results and the culture is ready for change.

- **Shake Up**—when significant structural changes must be made immediately to deliver the expected results and when the culture is not ready to change.

> If significant restructuring is deemed necessary during the transition period, the interim leader must be certain that the culture can accommodate the change. Key individuals must be on board or they will stymie progress by exploiting the interim leader's impermanence.
>
> Marta, an interim dean who assumed the role from her associate dean role, decided with her leadership team that the interim period was the appropriate time to engage in a much-needed restructuring of the college. The previous dean had started this process but dragged his feet and put off this difficult discussion for two years. Considerable effort over the one-year interim period was put into an open planning process for the restructuring. The provost endorsed the idea when Marta presented it but was not engaged in the process. When the time came for implementation, the faculty balked and questioned whether the new dean would support the proposed structure. The new permanent dean (who turned out to be not-so-permanent) was reluctant to take on the project, and the college continued with its archaic and inefficient structure for three more years. Marta's assessment was that the need for change was urgent but the culture was not ready for change. When the next dean came on board, she immediately embraced the work done during the interim period and used it as a framework for an open and successful restructuring.

Sometimes restructuring is upper management's primary charge to the interim leader. In these cases, the supervisor may feel that immediate attention is required to restructure the organization, likely because the current structure is leading to poor performance or dysfunction. It may also be the case that restructuring has been needed for some time and it will be easier for an interim to implement, leaving a smoother glide path for the permanent leader who follows. This authority can be critical in navigating the politics that commonly accompany restructuring.

Restructuring need not be full-scale reorganization. There are several options available to improve coordination and efficiency. Some of these options include:

- Strategically modifying selected reporting lines

- Joint reporting (not always a great idea, but sometimes it can be managed effectively)

- Appointing working groups or teams focused on specific coordination goals

- Structuring meetings that put the right people in the room to address specific topics

Finally, be prepared for managers of other units to come to you with proposals to either shift parts of your unit to theirs or vice versa. These might be legitimate proposals, but you need to proceed with caution. Just as there are people within your own unit who want to take advantage of the interim period to seize power and control, there will be others outside your unit with the same motives. They are likely shopping proposals that were tried earlier and rejected by your predecessor.

Chapter 7

MANAGING THE BUDGET

Prior to assuming the role of interim provost, I scheduled a meeting with my predecessor and brought along some budget documents I had requested during the front end. His response was a little surprising, "You aren't going to try to figure out the budget, are you?" At that point, I knew I was in trouble.

Budget and financial management present some unique challenges to the interim executive. The significance of these challenges will be influenced by one's experience in managing complex budgets, the degree to which budget management was emphasized during the previous administration, the competence of the finance and budget staff, and the organization's financial health. The interim leader must be able to quickly assess each of these factors and respond to any shortcomings identified.

THE IMPORTANCE OF TAKING ON THE BUDGET

Though budget and finance functions have always been important to successful higher education leadership, their relevance has risen significantly over the past two decades. A variety of forces have come together to increase the importance of acquiring and managing financial resources for both public and private institutions. This new fiscal context is framed by such factors as the long-term impacts of the Great Recession, the public sector's divestiture of responsibility for funding higher education, increasing government regulation and unfunded mandates, rising costs of goods and services, and greater competition in the higher education sector.

Although often potentially complex, you must manage the budget. An important aspect of leadership is allocating scarce resources, and these decisions cannot be made without a thorough knowledge of the budget. Mayhew (1979) notes that "budgets are really a statement of the purpose of an institution phrased in fiscal terms." Budgets and financial decision-making must align with mission and strategy.

Some within the higher education sector have been critical of the increased emphasis on finances in higher education administration. These critics note that bottom-line management has led to an erosion of educational quality and administrators "running colleges or universities like a business." It is true that excessive focus on the bottom line can be detrimental to delivering on the primary mission, but at the same time, its importance cannot be discounted. The fact is, financial considerations are one of most critical determinants of what is possible from a programming standpoint. While some members of the academy might find it blasphemous, colleges and universities are businesses (albeit most are not-for-profit businesses), with large public universities having annual budgets in the billions of dollars.

Most administrative positions in higher education carry with them the responsibility for budget management. Unfortunately, many executive leaders don't have training or experience in managing this important function. The assumption commonly made is that experience in program management, teaching, and research provides an operating knowledge in budget and finance. Unfortunately, this is often not the case.

Financial management was one function often cited by interim leaders as most challenging to grasp during their period of interim leadership. This is an interesting finding, as just about all these interim leaders were experienced administrators who had fiscal management responsibilities at the next level down in the university hierarchy. Drilling down on their responses, most pointed to the time and energy required to gain a firm appreciation of the fiscal situation and understand internal budget processes. In cases where interim leaders are stepping up from a level below—e.g., department chair to interim dean, associate vice president to interim vice president—the fiscal complexity often increases severalfold. Of course, interims who have worked within the organization have a distinct advantage in that they are familiar with the current policies, practices, and nomenclature.

GETTING A HANDLE ON FISCAL AFFAIRS

At first blush, one might think that gaining an understanding of the new unit's financial affairs simply involves sitting down and reviewing available budgets and financial reports—i.e., looking at the numbers. Unfortunately, it is a little more complicated than that. To truly obtain a working knowledge of fiscal affairs requires developing an understanding of an organization's budget history and culture, its budget policies and procedures, the people involved in budget management, and finally, the numbers.

Understanding Budget History and Culture

Like every other aspect of your new organization, the unit's financial and budget history serves to define the culture that you inherit. Every unit is characterized by a set of customs, values, and standards that define how it engages in financial and budget management activities. For example, some units have a history of tight fiscal control with rigid approval processes while others practice looser oversight and provide managers significant day-to-day autonomy in managing their budgets. Similarly, some units have very structured and codified processes for managing budgets while others rely on practices and processes established by the longtime culture of the organization and preferences of past leaders.

It is important to understand this culture because a rapid switch to new operating policies and processes can create substantial confusion and pushback. This is not to say that changes shouldn't occur, but understanding the working environment will allow for a more seamless transition to a new normal.

Cleaning up past financial mismanagement can be one of the first tasks thrust upon a new interim leader. Sometimes inherited financial challenges are not just about overspending the budget but are rooted in the absence of appropriate financial processes and controls.

An interim vice president of finance, Gloria was recruited into the position from outside the university after retiring from an institution of greater size and complexity. The president hired her following the retirement of the longtime vice president shortly after the president assumed the office. During her early assessment, Gloria quickly discovered some concerning things about the financial processes and controls in place. Most notably, several units were routinely overspending. Although budget processes were in place, vice presidents and deans had little accountability to these budgets and several regularly overspent their annual allocation, resulting in large accumulated deficits.

> Gloria immediately put into place policies requiring quarterly budget reviews and strict adherence to annual budgets. These directives were initially met with resistance because they translated to difficult decisions by unit leaders who were forced to cut expenditures below levels that would have generated additional deficits. Units with significant accumulated deficits were required to develop and gain approval of a three-year fiscal recovery plan. These were important first steps in renewing the university's overall financial health.

Understanding Budget Processes

A key outcome of the assessment process in the front end and the first thirty days is to gain clarity on the budget and fiscal management processes used. These processes include policies and procedures employed both within the unit as well as the entire organization. The latter define how the unit engages with finance and budget officials responsible for fiscal affairs across the university. The former dictate how budget planning and control is executed within the unit.

For the most part, an interim leader is primarily concerned about short-run budget management. Unless specifically directed, an interim leader has neither the time nor the clout to make significant changes to the budget model used by the organization. Therefore, fiscal management primarily involves making decisions within the existing budget framework.

As noted in previous discussions, the length and slope of the learning curve will be greatly dependent upon previous administrative experience. Interim leaders who have been promoted from within the unit are likely to have a good understanding of policies and processes within the unit; however, they might not have much experience with university-level engagement. If the interim is transferred from a similar position in another part of the university, the opposite may be true. And, of course, the interim coming from outside the university has no familiarity with either.

Upon entering some of the administrative positions I have held, I was surprised at how poor a handle the organization had on budget and finance. Over half of interim leaders surveyed had similar experiences. For most, this meant that the budget and financial management processes and controls they inherited were inadequate to plan and monitor critical variables such as the assorted revenues and expenditures of the organization. Others encountered a lack of knowledge within the administration regarding the overall financial health of the organization.

Budget processes can differ significantly across institutions and among units within an institution. Before delving into budget management, it is important to have a solid understanding of the budget culture, policies, and practices used in the past.

Harriet, a former interim dean, came into the position a couple of months prior to the new fiscal year. At a college leadership meeting during her first month, she distributed a budget packet describing the steps to be employed in developing the college's annual operating budget, budget forms to be submitted, and so on. She developed these materials from the processes used in another college where she had previously served.

When Harriet distributed the materials, she was met with consternation on the faces of her department chairs and directors, and quickly recognized that the group had never been asked to participate in a budget development exercise. The previous dean basically handled the construction of the annual budget with the chief financial officer using an incremental budgeting approach—i.e., starting with the previous year's budget and making incremental adjustments to account for changes made over the past year and any priorities for the next year. She was forced to backtrack and guide the leadership team through a process of formulating a shared approach to budget development that was simpler than her initial proposal. A better understanding and appreciation of the college's budget culture would have allowed Harriet to provide more time for the chairs and directors to adapt and more fully and confidently participate in the budget process.

A key first step is to sit down with your finance officer for a crash course in the fiscal management processes used up to that point. Is there an annual budget? Yes, sometimes higher education units are being operated without a legitimate annual budget. What reports are routinely generated? How frequently are these reports presented to the leader? How are subunits within the organization budgeted and held accountable to these budgets?

The goal here is not to conduct a complete financial audit of the organization but rather to gain an appreciation of budget policies, processes, and practices that impact the administrative environment in which you will be operating. Oftentimes, these policies will define some of the boundaries of decisions that can be made in leading the unit.

Assessing the Capabilities of the Fiscal Team

Like everything within an organization, people are the key to successful financial management. Taking stock of fiscal affairs requires assessing the capabilities of those responsible for budget and fiscal management. This includes the chief financial officer (CFO), the fiscal staff, and managers with budget responsibilities.

A good place to start is with your CFO. These positions have several titles, but the CFO title is used here to refer to the person who leads finance and budget for the organization and reports directly to the executive leader. For a dean, this may be the college budget director. For a president, it may be the vice president for finance.

Successful budget and financial management require a trusting and respectful relationship with your CFO. Just like the executive assistant position discussed in chapter 4, your CFO can be an extraordinary resource in managing the financial dimensions of the position, providing critical information for decision-making and allowing you to focus on the right things. Building this trust early is imperative for executing a successful interim term. The CFO can also serve as an important conduit of financial information to those responsible for fiscal management at lower levels of the organization—e.g., departments, centers, and schools within a college.

Determining the team's capabilities also includes assessing the budget savvy of unit leaders responsible for managing budgets—e.g., department chairs for an interim dean. In the above case, the interim dean did not spend enough time doing her homework and discovered that unit leaders did not have the level of budget experience needed to manage the budget the way she envisioned.

Interviews with a couple of experienced finance officers who have worked with multiple interim leaders revealed that the introduction of a new executive leader can generate uncertainty and dramatically change the rhythm by which they execute their day-to-day operations. Not surprisingly, finance officers interviewed noted significant variation across interim leaders in terms of interest in financial management, preferred format for financial reports, and ability to understand financial information. As with executive assistants, the greatest challenge for these finance officers occurred when they switched between executives with dramatically different leadership styles and appreciation for fiscal management. For example, moving from a leader who engages the finance officer as an equal member of the leadership team to one who views the finance officer as simply an information provider can be very frustrating to a CFO.

Some suggestions offered by experienced CFOs to ease the transition were:

- **Schedule regular one-on-one meetings.** For whatever reason, finance officers often get shortchanged when it comes to time with executive leaders, particularly leaders who aren't too interested in fiscal affairs.

- **Prioritize information.** Focus on high-dollar, time-sensitive issues first.

- **Pop in on your finance officer when a topic is top-of-mind.** Some of the best information sharing sessions are ad hoc.

- **Keep asking questions until you understand the information provided.** It is not helpful to the CFO if you nod in agreement but don't really understand the report set in front of you. CFOs need feedback to be most helpful to you moving forward.

- **Include finance officers in leadership meetings.** It will help both of you better connect the dots between program and budget.

Include yourself in the assessment of people's capabilities. Based on your assessment of those providing financial support and the complexity of the unit's finances, you need to make a quick assessment of your own abilities to manage this area of the position. Seek help from others to acquire the needed skills, information, and competencies.

Understanding the Numbers

The final step in assessing the organization's fiscal management is to get a better handle on the unit's actual financial performance. Ideally, you were able to gain a general appreciation of how funds are allocated and the unit's financial health through your review of reports and conversations during the front end. Now it's time to dig a little deeper.

An important first question to answer is whether the current allocation of funds is reflective of the organization's mission and goals. As an interim, you have a unique opportunity to ask and answer this question without being influenced by history or momentum for the status quo. As noted previously, actions communicate louder than words, and there may be no stronger message during your interim period than decisions made concerning how funds are allocated across the institution.

A frequent frustration of new executive leaders is not being able to understand the financial reports provided to them. Executive leaders who actively manage fiscal matters normally have some specific preferences about how financial information is presented. A portion of early meetings with the unit's CFO should be devoted to working through current financial reports and budgets. It is useful to work with those currently being used to determine if they will provide the information necessary to manage the unit. Give the CFO the opportunity to explain the rationale for each report and its format. Ask the CFO to identify any concerns about the unit's financial performance and opportunities for improvement. A competent CFO is always thinking about these considerations and will have much to say on the topic.

It is important that you communicate your needs and expectations to your CFO. If the reports do not provide you with clear and timely information, the two of you will need to collaborate to develop reports that work for you. It is well understood that your financial information needs will differ from your predecessor's; a competent CFO is prepared to adapt.

When drilling down into the numbers, a balancing act is required. The interim executive should not get mired in the financial details; that is the job of the CFO and finance staff. During my time as provost, I encountered a couple of deans who literally were completing all of their college's budgeting on self-prepared spreadsheets. In my opinion, this is neither good budget management nor sound leadership and leads to misallocation of time and energy, lack of empowerment of the finance team, and fiscal mismanagement. The level of fiscal scrutiny and oversight required is case-dependent and influenced by what is discovered in your early assessment activities. Obviously, if inadequate financial controls are in place or signs of poor financial performance are identified, additional scrutiny is required.

MANAGING BUDGETS

There are several types of budgets that executive leaders must manage, including operating, capital, auxiliary, and special funds budgets (Barr and McClellan 2010).

Managing the Operating Budget

Management of the operating budget is a never-ending task of any university executive. In fact, university executives understand that you are never managing just one operating budget; while you are managing revenues and expenditures of the current budget cycle, you may be closing the past budget year and planning for the next one.

Common steps involved in a typical annual operating budget cycle are shown in Figure 7.1. Some of these steps are sequential while others may occur simultaneously. As illustrated, many of the activities within the budget cycle occur outside the fiscal year. Prior to the initiation of a new fiscal year, budget preparation activities must be completed. Steps involved in budget preparation include: (1) analyzing previous budget performance, (2) establishing the internal budget preparation process, (3) reviewing internal proposals from units, (4) preparing a draft budget, (5) vetting the budget with unit leaders, and (6) finalizing the budget and gaining needed approvals. Through the fiscal year, performance is carefully monitored, and the current budget is modified to reflect any changing conditions that require revision of revenues or expenditures.

Most interim executives don't have the luxury of entering their position at the beginning of the fiscal year and might start at any point in this cycle. The trick is to jump on the track and catch up with the fast-moving train that is not slowing down while you climb the learning curve. Some questions to ask:

- What decisions for the current budget cycle are irreversible?

- Are there any past decisions that need to be revisited?

- How is the organization and its various units performing relative to budgeted revenues and expenditures?

- What are the critical decisions coming up for the next budget cycle?

If your preliminary assessment determines that sound budget policies and practices are in place, you can likely utilize the same budget process that was employed the previous year, with perhaps some minor tweaks. Unit leaders are accustomed to the steps used in the past and the timeline. There is little value in changing. If that is not the case, then additional time and effort will be required to inculcate a new budget process, and initiation of the budget preparation phase should occur earlier. The internal budget process within the unit should have a clear timeline and be straightforward and unambiguous; everyone involved should be told how and when decisions will be made.

As noted earlier, budgets are a statement of an organization's purpose and priorities phrased in fiscal terms. If the budget is not aligned with

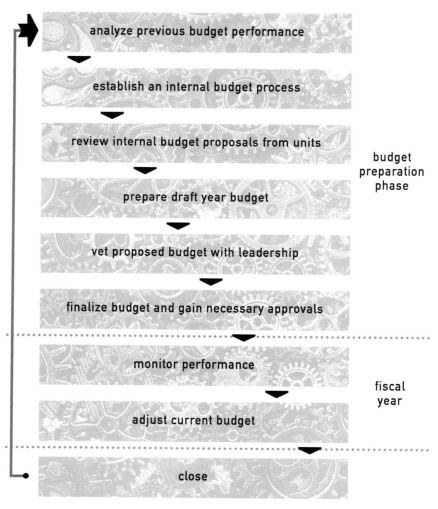

Figure 7.1. Typical Steps for Managing a Budget Cycle

priorities, you can use the budget development process to begin realigning resources to match the hierarchy of needs. One common approach is to ask that unit-level budget requests reflect ongoing priorities as well as any new priorities identified for the interim period.

Managing Capital, Special Funds, and Auxiliary Budgets

Capital budgets reflect revenues and expenses associated with large, multiyear capital projects. These projects are typically administrated at the institutional level, and the interim executive has likely inherited a financial position that reflects the long-term planning of the previous incumbent. It is important to become aware of these past considerations and, at a minimum, maintain the organization's place within the institution's capital budget.

In its purest form, an auxiliary enterprise in higher education is a unit that is fully self-supporting, meaning that it does not receive support from the operating budget. These enterprises have proliferated in recent years as colleges and universities have sought alternative enterprises and revenue streams to supplement traditional sources. Auxiliary enterprises are entities for which improper spending can occur in the absence of appropriate controls. The main thing to look for here is evidence that appropriate controls are in place to assure that institutional policies are being adhered to in managing these enterprises.

Special funds budgets are established for designated programs, and they indicate resources and expenses for such activities. A common reason for establishing budgets for these programs is that available funds have restricted use for a specific purpose (Goldstein 2005). A common example are special funds budgets for tracking revenues and expenses associated with an endowed gift fund. Misuse of special funds has generated some embarrassing situations for a handful of presidents and deans in recent years, so you should look for any potential land mines in this area.

DEALING WITH DIFFICULT FISCAL SITUATIONS

Some interim leaders inherit dire financial circumstances that present a whole other set of challenges. Unfortunately, these situations have increased in frequency, given the economic forces that have faced higher education over the past two decades. Almost every interim leader interviewed noted financial stress as one of the key challenges faced during their interim term. Several noted that the financial condition of the unit was more dire than was communicated to them by the administrator who hired them. In most of these cases, the hiring administrator was unaware of the degree of the problem until the interim came on board and started looking into it.

Too often, interim leaders are forced, knowingly or unknowingly, to tackle difficult financial situations. In these circumstances, the goals are to develop an accurate assessment of the situation and a multi-year plan to move the organization to financial stability.

Frank, an interim dean, was promoted from within the college after the incumbent dean's resignation a few years after the Great Recession. The college had struggled to recover from the budget cuts of prior years, and one of the charges given to the interim dean by the provost was to develop a financial recovery plan. What Frank quickly discovered was that the situation was much more dire than anyone knew. Financial records were inaccurate, and units were not accountable to annual budgets. Not only had large deficits accumulated over several years, but large financial commitments had been made to fund faculty start-ups, leaving huge encumbrances that were going to hit the college budget over the coming two years.

Frank labored tirelessly over the first three months of the transition period to get a more accurate picture of the financial situation. He worked with his leadership team and the provost to develop a multi-year recovery plan and communicated it to the faculty and staff. Several unit leaders pushed back, either not believing the situation or resisting accountability to help clean up the problem. Two unit leaders resigned and one was replaced, providing new leadership that was willing to take on the challenge. As a result of Frank's one and a half years of interim leadership, the college was able to develop and initiate a fiscal recovery plan and hire a highly qualified dean to lead the college and continue financial recovery efforts.

Interim leaders are often faced with continuing a series of difficult budget decisions that have faced their predecessors. Again, impermanence has value—the interim's temporary status and perceived neutrality can be used to come in and take a fresh look at budget decisions. Difficult choices can be made that might be politically intractable for the permanent leader.

Patience is an important quality for an interim leader to demonstrate in managing these situations. Most financial messes were not created in a year, and it will typically take multiple years to work through a recovery. The interim leader's job is to identify the problem and set the organization on a road to financial health.

Each financial situation is unique, and there is no magic formula for working through times of financial stress. Six steps to consider in developing a financial recovery plan are outlined in Figure 7.2.

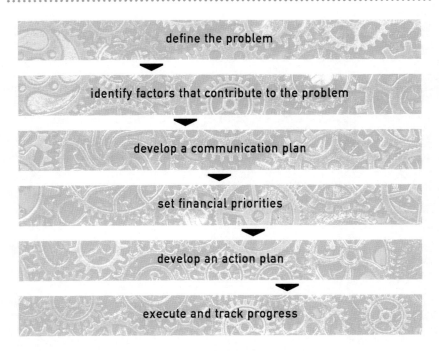

Figure 7.2. Steps for Developing a Financial Recovery Plan

1. Define the problem.

The first step to overcoming a financial crisis is to identify the primary problem that is causing difficulties. If accurate financial information is not available, additional work is required to gain a complete assessment of the financial picture. In the above case, additional analysis revealed not only an immediate problem but also financial commitments into the future that would have longer term impacts.

2. Identify key factors that contributed to the problem.

Before developing a recovery plan, it is critical to know the primary factors that contributed to the situation. Financial problems are generally an indication of a larger issue; to come up with long-run solutions, you must identify the root causes of the financial troubles. These factors can be internal to the unit or external and completely out of the executive leader's control. Internal sources could include things like poor programmatic decisions, failure to adjust to changing economic forces, excessive spending, inaccurate revenue and expenditure forecasting, or absence of proper fiscal controls. In the above case, a primary contributing factor was the failure to hold unit leaders accountable for their budgets.

3. Develop a communication plan.

As repeated throughout this book, communication is an important element to successful executive leadership. Once the financial situation is well-defined, it is important to communicate the nature of the problem. Remedying the situation will impact people and programs throughout the organization, and everyone will need to prepare for the consequences.

Transparency is always important when dealing with challenging fiscal situations in higher education, but it is even more critical for the interim. The faculty, staff, and administration must have confidence in the decisions being made; thus, a solid communication plan that addresses the how, what, when, and why of budgetary decisions is critical.

Budget transparency can be difficult because oftentimes the issues, fiscal responses, and their rationale are more complicated than can be explained in an email correspondence. Some interim leaders interviewed, particularly deans, successfully used budget advisory committees to improve communication and transparency. Such committees provide a forum for the interim leader to explain the fiscal situation in more detail and gain input from internal stakeholders on potential administrative responses.

4. Set financial priorities.

As is the case with most situations facing interim leaders, it is critical to set priorities. Financial priorities help you make tough financial decisions. Most of the time, steps taken to address extreme financial circumstances carry with them both programmatic and financial trade-offs. For example, eliminating staff positions might yield reductions in salary and benefits, but the action could also adversely impact financial controls across the organization. In addition, these trade-offs can pit the short run against the long run. For example, a decision to implement a hiring freeze to improve short-run cash flow can adversely affect long-term grant revenues.

5. Develop an action plan.

Any action plan should be jointly developed by the entire leadership team. Financial recovery actions must reach into all areas of the organization, so it is important that buy-in is achieved throughout. The plan should define metrics for measuring progress and a timetable for milestone achievement. An interim leader should build as much flexibility into the plan as possible to allow the successor the opportunity to refine the plan on assuming leadership of the unit.

6. Execute and track progress.

Once the recovery plan is developed, it's time to put it into action. A critical component of execution is measuring progress against milestones and reporting progress to the organization.

BUDGET PITFALLS

There are several behaviors that create challenges for the people responsible for budget management. This short summary provides a list of problems that I have encountered. An incoming interim leader should look out for these and avoid practicing them so that you do not hand problems off to your successor.

1. Handshake deals

A lot of important work at colleges and universities is done with little formally documented communication. These handshake deals can be very difficult to unwind when the leader leaves the university or is no longer available to consult. All agreements involving financial commitments should be codified and easily accessible, regardless of personnel changes.

2. Failing to specify a time frame for financial commitments

As you inventory past financial commitments, you might find some that are documented in writing but have no time frame. No commitment goes on for perpetuity, so make certain that any commitments include a specified time frame, or at a minimum, a time frame for when the agreement will be revisited.

3. Ad hoc spending

In the case referenced earlier in the chapter, most of the executives who routinely overspent their annual operating budgets began the fiscal year with a balanced budget projection. Budget overruns occurred because they engaged in ad hoc spending without commensurate expenditure reductions or revenue increases. Leaders must be disciplined to avoid engaging in this activity.

4. Overestimating revenue

It is much easier to balance a projected budget by overestimating revenue than by reducing planned expenditures. Overoptimistic revenue forecasts fueled by blind optimism can be a common cause of deficit spending. Revenue forecasts should be conservative and based on realistic assumptions.

5. Failing to account for impacts on others

Budget decisions are not made in a vacuum, and every decision can have both intended and unintended consequences. Executive leaders must not only consider the consequences of a decision on their own unit but also think about the consequences on other units as well as the greater institution. For example, the impacts of a decision by the office of student affairs to discontinue a centrally provided service can trickle down to academic colleges who might be forced to provide the service locally.

6. Failing to account for hidden costs

Proper financial decision-making requires all costs be factored into the analysis. Universities are replete with hidden costs that are often not considered when initiating a program or project. Consider the simple example of hiring a new staff position. The cost of this hire is much greater than salary and benefits. Additional costs such as office space, equipment and supplies, IT support, staff support, and so forth should all be factored into the decision.

A personal pet peeve of mine is failure to consider another form of hidden costs—opportunity costs. I cannot count the number of times an academic leader has come to me with a proposed new academic program and stated that they could deliver it with little to no additional cost because "we already have the faculty and staff in place." This reasoning fails to recognize the opportunity cost of these peoples' time; that is, time allocated to the new program will have to come at the expense of some current use of their time.

7. Delaying difficult decisions

Some leaders would rather avoid the difficulty associated with addressing a financial problem than take it on directly. Deficits do not disappear, and overspending does not rectify itself. Avoidance strategies typically only exacerbate the problem. Many interims quickly encounter fiscal challenges that have been kicked down the road by previous leaders. Addressing these situations is one of the best gifts you can give a successor.

8. Overreliance on the previous budget when making funding decisions

Many institutions and units within them employ incremental budget development, which simply involves minor tweaks to the previous year's budget. In the dynamic world that is higher education today, this status quo approach will ultimately lead to misallocation of funds and limit responsiveness to emerging opportunities.

9. Failing to plan for the end

Many revenue streams in higher education are only realized for a short time period. Grants and other extramural funding are the most obvious examples. When the grant is received, facilities are dedicated and personnel are hired to achieve the project's objectives. However, when the grant reaches its conclusion, there is often considerable handwringing over how to continue these activities. Planning for the end of the grant should be initiated at the beginning of the grant.

Transparency is a critical element to any financial recovery plan introduced by an interim leader. The problems were not created by you, but addressing problems often requires some significant changes in financial management practices and difficult "belt-tightening exercises." The key is to be up front with regard to defining the problem and the steps necessary to move toward financial recovery.

When I became interim president, I succeeded a beloved president who passed away while in office. He was an inspiring and visionary leader and the most influential mentor of my administrative career. Like many visionaries, he was a "thirty-thousand-foot leader" and did not like to scrutinize budgets. When I assumed the interim role, I began to ask budget-related questions and was concerned about what we discovered. The problem wasn't that the president ignored the budget—it was that no one seemed to be proactively monitoring the budget. This problem was compounded by the recent retirement of the associate vice president for finance.

After about a month of intense budget scrutiny and working with a young, talented finance officer, we had some troublesome news to report to the board of regents—the institution's overall financial situation was much worse than imagined. Large capital commitments made over the previous two years, combined with state budget reductions, changes in accounting rules, and tuition shortfalls had created a situation where financial reserves were forecast to significantly decline over the coming three years. The entire interim period as well as the two subsequent years were dedicated to intense budget scrutiny and spending reductions. Probably the most significant contribution of my time as interim president was identifying the problem and kick-starting fiscal recovery.

Chapter 8

MANAGING EXTERNAL RELATIONS

A critical and growing portion of any university executive's responsibilities is to advance external relations. One cannot read a notice of vacancy for an executive leadership position that does not place a heavy emphasis on development and external relations.

Two terms commonly used to describe external relations activities are development and advancement. Development refers largely to fundraising. Advancement is a broader term that encompasses all functions related to advancing the cause of a program or institution externally. Traditionally, the advancement model relates to the integrated functions of development, alumni relations, and communications. More recently, some institutions have broadened the concept to include government relations, industry relations, public relations, and other functions involved in working with external stakeholders.

External stakeholders take on many forms: donors, alumni, business and industry leaders, policy makers, and community leaders. While all executive leaders have external relations in their portfolio, involvement with each of these groups will differ across positions. Obviously, the president will be intimately involved with all of these groups, while the vice president for information technology might focus on engagement with business and industry leaders and policy makers. Deans are likely to be most engaged with alumni, business and industry leaders, and donors.

COORDINATING THE TRANSITION WITH EXTERNAL STAKEHOLDERS

A common mistake of interim executives is to dedicate all of their energies to pressing internal affairs and overlook the importance of reaching out to external stakeholders to ease any concerns they might have about the transition. Internal affairs tend to be more urgent, but they are not all-important (or at least not as important as some external affairs).

External relations must be coordinated with all personnel and offices working within this area. For an interim president, this means calling together directors and vice presidents responsible for such areas as development, alumni affairs, government relations, marketing, and communications. Everyone with responsibilities in external affairs should be part of developing an integrated strategy. Similarly for deans, all members of the college leadership team responsible for external relations should be part of developing an integrated strategy for the college.

Development of an integrated strategy for engaging external stakeholders is an exercise in prioritization. The new leader must not only prioritize across functions—e.g., development, government relations, alumni relations—but also across stakeholders within a function area. Having a firm thirty-day plan and an outcome-driven action plan for the interim period will provide the guidance needed to make these decisions.

Don't be surprised to find leaders responsible for areas such as development, alumni relations, industry relations, and government relations all competing for your time. They are well-intentioned, but individually they likely don't have the perspective to objectively evaluate time allocation. For interim presidents and perhaps other positions with large external roles, there will likely be a significant number of requests to attend external events. Establishing a set of guidelines for prioritizing external activities is a useful exercise for the group. It is very helpful to get all these leaders together in a room and hash out criteria for filtering external opportunities and governing scheduling decisions.

The timetable of activities for reaching out to external stakeholders should be a key component of the communication plan outlined in chapter 2. Phasing is critical, and stakeholders should be prioritized for contact, with the highest priority receiving early and high-touch communications. The initial message is simple and straightforward—the organization is in good hands and moving forward. Emphasize priorities that transcend a single leader.

This work should be initiated during the front end because some key external stakeholders should be contacted prior to the announcement of the interim leader's appointment. The importance of these early contacts increases with the level of the executive position in the university hierarchy.

The interim leader's external communication strategy should be carefully crafted, beginning during the front end and continuing through the transition period. Work with members of the leadership team to prioritize contacts with donors, alumni, policy makers, and business and industry leaders.

When the death of our president was imminent and I was selected by the board of regents to serve as interim president, our leadership team did an incredible job of coordinating the announcement of the leadership transition. Tragically, this announcement accompanied the news of the death of our beloved president. The announcement was successfully executed because it was developed and coordinated by several key leadership team members—government relations, alumni affairs, student affairs, development, chancellors of branch campuses, and communications. In the days leading up to the president's death, we developed a list of all key external and internal stakeholders and divided these names among members of the leadership team who had the strongest relationship with each. Key talking points were developed and customized for each individual. When we received news of the president's death, we initiated the calling tree and connected with over one hundred key stakeholders within two hours, reaching most before others contacted them or they heard the news in the media. A press release went out immediately, and as a result, I was able to conduct interviews with ten different print, television, and radio media outlets within two days.

Most communication plans at the beginning of the transition period need not be this rapid, but this case does demonstrate the type of planning required to execute a smooth transition with external stakeholders.

WORKING WITH DONORS

Development is an important responsibility of almost every executive leader within a college or university. Unfortunately, it is also an area where interim leaders often struggle. The importance of "friendraising" and fundraising differs across executive positions, with deans and presidents carrying the greatest responsibility in this area.

Some academic leaders enjoy development and are highly successful at it. Others tolerate it but engage reluctantly or cautiously. Still others abhor it and make every effort to avoid it. Not surprisingly, the first group is most effective; they are sometimes referred to as development presidents or development deans.

Many interim executive leaders have substantial development experience, so this part of their new role is not foreign to them. The task for these individuals is to make the transition to a new organizational vision and a new group of donors. Several interim deans interviewed noted that development was one of the most challenging functions of their new position. Not surprisingly, those who struggled did not have a lot of experience with development in their previous roles and were not actively engaged in development activities with the former dean.

The first step toward success in development is simply to realize that the activity must be a priority. It is easy for an interim leader to become so preoccupied with learning the ins and outs of a new position and putting out day-to-day brushfires that development is not given the attention it deserves. Allocating time, energy, and thought to development requires discipline. It is important to carve out a specific number of days on your monthly calendar to dedicate to development activities.

The interim leader must also realize that philanthropic momentum tends to wane during leadership transitions. Prospective donors may be reluctant to give because of their personal relationship with the outgoing leader or in anticipation of a new leader. Celebrating the legacy of the outgoing leader and funding the next permanent leader's transition are two messages that may resonate with donors during the interim period.

Among interim leaders interviewed, the key variables in moving forward quickly and effectively in development were their familiarity with donors and the degree to which they were previously involved in development. For example, interim presidents who were actively engaged with donors as a provost were able to achieve quick success with key university-level donors.

Working with the Development Team

An early priority, perhaps during the front end and certainly during the first thirty days, is to meet with your development leader to get the "lay of the land" with respect to fundraising efforts. Again, the amount of new information shared in this meeting will depend on the degree to which the interim leader was engaged in development activities with the constituency of their new position. Communicate to the development leader that you will make fundraising a priority and begin to create a plan for development activities during the interim period. Take some time to review the organization's development vision and fundraising priorities. It is critical that the new leader is in sync with the development team in these areas.

A strong development team will assure that the portion of your time spent friendraising and fundraising will be productive. Healthy partnerships between a leader and the development staff start with mutual trust and respect. Many of the tips presented in chapter 4 also apply to working with these professionals.

Hunt (2012) provides four expectations you should have of your development team:

- **They should identify opportunities.** The team should bring forth creative ideas and prospective donors regularly.

- **They should work independently.** Development professionals work independently and do not rely on the executive to lead fundraising activities.

- **They should deploy you wisely.** You don't need to see every donor and every donor does not need to see you. Prioritizing potential visits and events for maximum impact is a critical role of the development staff.

- **They should tell you the unvarnished truth.** Not everything goes as planned, and development staff need to be candid in explaining how well they perceive you are doing with a donor relationship.

What should the development team expect of you?

- **Clearly set your priorities and expectations.** Again, you and the development team need to be in sync; the executive leader's most important role is to articulate a clear vision and priorities, and remain consistent.

- **Let the development team do its work.** As noted above, development professionals are expected to work independently, and you need to avoid unnecessary oversight. Also, guard them from nondevelopment activities—e.g., event planning.

- **Make yourself available and reliable.** There is nothing worse for a development professional than to schedule a donor visit, only to have the leader cancel out at the last minute.

- **Provide regular communication.** The development leader should be
firmly entrenched in the organization's leadership team and kept in
the loop about all major initiatives and activities.

The key to effective development for any executive leader is proper time
allocation. You will never have enough time for development, so it is critical that you be very strategic and intentional about your external events
and one-on-one visits.

Prospect Management

Complete an inventory of all key prospects. At the university level, key
prospects can be divided into three tiers: Tier I, 25 to 50 prospects requiring a hands-on communication strategy; Tier II, 50 to 100 prospects
requiring personal contact, which may take a different form and may not
be as immediate as Tier I; and Tier III, the next 100 to 250 prospects. These
guidelines are for a comprehensive public university; for smaller colleges
and universities, vice presidential areas, or colleges within a university, the
numbers will likely be much smaller.

A discussion of each prospect requiring immediate attention should
be held with the development director. What stage of the cultivation
process are you at with each prospect? What was your predecessor's role
in this relationship? Has a monetary ask been identified for the prospect?

Develop a strategy for each Tier I and Tier II prospect during the
interim period. The most important goal is to assure that you maintain
the trust and confidence of each prospect. You should aspire to keep all
prospects moving through the cultivation pipeline. Development is an
area where you should be focused primarily on setting up your successor; therefore, success is not necessarily measured by dollars raised but by
contacts made, advancement achieved with donors, and gifts cued up for
the incoming permanent leader.

All Tier I prospects should be contacted within the thirty-day period,
at least by phone but preferably in person. Trust and confidence are best
secured by eye-to-eye contact. The message is clear and simple—the organization is in good hands and moving forward. Don't be afraid to share
personal information about yourself, as another goal of these initial visits is
for the donor to become comfortable with you and your commitment to

the institution. A strategy should be developed for Tier II candidates that might involve either a form of communication other than a face-to-face meeting or a meeting with someone else from the institution.

A written correspondence should go out to all investors in the university or college, large and small, once again reinforcing the message that the organization—e.g., university, college—is moving forward with its unchanging mission and initiatives. For interim deans, provosts, and vice presidents, the university president can be a stable and trusted conveyor of this message.

Relationships with donors are often very personal. In some situations, the prospect's relationship with the institution may be almost entirely through interaction with the previous leader. This is particularly the case with leaders who exercise near-complete control over donor relationships. These can be tricky situations, as the departure of the previous leader can translate to a large setback in trust and confidence.

It is not always the case that the departure of an executive leader translates to a delay or loss of a significant gift. The interim leader must exercise the patience to visit with each potential donor, reestablish trust, and assess their readiness to continue the cultivation process. Ultimately, this work will lead to finalizing the gift during the transition period or teeing up the gift for the incoming permanent leader.

A former interim president, Luke shared a case where the university had been working with a donor on a major naming opportunity when the president died suddenly while in office. Then the provost, Luke was promoted to the role of interim president. Fortunately, the potential gift was within the academic enterprise, so Luke had been involved in cultivating the gift in his role as provost. After an appropriate grieving period, he approached the donor with the same project. The key was securing the donor's trust and assuring him that the institution would deliver on the vision. In this case, the loss of the president had actually strengthened the donor's resolve to make the project happen. Luke was able to secure an eight-figure gift from the donor.

It is critical to identify the donor's passion. Donors typically do not give to people; they give to ideas and visions they are passionate about (Cannon 2011). The previous leader was simply the person who delivered the message, so you need to identify the donor's points of passion and get on message as quickly as possible.

As noted earlier, a primary development goal of an interim leader is to provide a running start for the incoming leader, who requires philanthropic funding to support his or her emerging vision, achieve immediate impact, and gather institutional momentum. Early investors will play a critical role in the success of new leaders and be among the first to engage with them. Lining up volunteers to assist will provide an important service to the new leader.

Another important means of supporting incoming leaders is to tee up gifts to support their transition. Astute development directors will be acutely aware of this goal and provide guidance throughout the interim period to build a bundle of unannounced gifts, pledges, and teed-up gifts. Optimally, new permanent leaders will be able to roll out pieces of this bundle in their initial months in office, thus establishing credibility and success—i.e., "early wins."

While each situation will be unique, the list of possible activities provided in Table 8.1 should be useful in framing a development plan.

Table 8.1. LIST OF POTENTIAL DEVELOPMENT ACTIVITIES FOR INTERIM PERIOD

✓ Identify and communicate development as a priority
✓ Review current development vision and priorities
✓ Meet with development leader
✓ Develop primary development message with team
✓ Inventory key prospects
✓ Make immediate and personal contact with Tier I prospects
✓ Initial message to all investors in the college or university
✓ Make personal contact with Tier II prospects
✓ Develop a strategy for continuing cultivation of all key prospects
✓ Develop a plan outlining development events, activities, and visits for the interim period
✓ Execute the plan

WORKING WITH OTHER EXTERNAL STAKEHOLDERS

The broad definition of advancement includes not only development and alumni relations but also such functions as government relations, industry relations, public relations, and other activities related to work with external stakeholders. Of course, the importance of each of these groups will differ by executive position.

Alumni and Friends

Alumni are an important stakeholder group for interim deans, provosts, and presidents. Again, the critical message to get out to this group is that the organization is in good hands. As quickly as possible, send out a communication that introduces yourself, articulates the primary message you have crafted for the first thirty days, and provides a timeline for finding a permanent successor.

Past interim presidents stressed the importance of getting out and defining yourself as the leader of the institution. There are likely many alumni events scheduled, and these can be an effective venue for alumni and friends to engage with a new interim leader. Using a multipronged approach as outlined in the first thirty days communication plan is critical.

For interim presidents, the media will likely reach out to seek interviews. This is an excellent opportunity to capture earned media coverage for the university. The media will be friendly and want to get to know you better as a person and a leader. Again, keeping the message simple and reinforcing the core idea of stability in mission are the goals of these conversations.

Advisory councils and alumni groups can be used as important allies. For interim deans, one of your early calls should be to the leaders of external stakeholder groups—e.g., the college advisory council. Leaders of these groups will soon be getting calls from concerned alumni and friends, and you want them messaging positively and accurately. Members of the advisory and alumni groups should receive a communication prior to a broad correspondence to all alumni. You want volunteer leaders to feel valued and informed.

One area in which interim presidents typically have little experience is intercollegiate athletics. Obviously, the issues and complexities of this area depend on the level at which the institution's intercollegiate athletics programs compete. For universities competing at the Division I level, this area can yield some challenging external situations and surprises. It is also an area where many alumni have the strongest connection to the university and demonstrate considerable passion. Presidents of these institutions know all too well that athletics can be problematic in a number of ways, but it is also an area that can be utilized to spread goodwill toward the institution. Interim presidents interviewed noted the importance of frequent communication with the athletics director and getting up to speed on any potential issues that may present themselves in the interim period.

During my first several months as interim president, I made it a point to attend several away football games. This was something my predecessor did not often engage in, but being in front of one-thousand-plus alumni at pregame events proved extremely useful in communicating our message. I also chose to sit in the stands with our fans as opposed to using the suite reserved for the visiting team. Obviously, this strategy took time, but in hindsight the benefit-cost ratio was enormous. Alumni remembered this visibility and were still referencing it in conversations several years later.

Business and Industry

Key business and industry partners also represent important touch points. Engagement with the private sector has become increasingly important to higher education institutions in developing productive research partnerships and professional development opportunities for students and faculty, soliciting curriculum advice, and providing extramural funding. Colleges typically have several established relationships with industry leaders, and interim deans should work with their leadership team to identify these contacts. Business leaders tend to be more understanding of leadership change because they often experience turnover within their own firms, so the conversation will likely serve as an opportunity to introduce yourself and provide assurance that the partnership will continue.

Business leaders often do not understand the process by which higher education institutions hire executive leaders. They typically find the search process for a new dean, for example, to be tedious and time-consuming. It is helpful to explain the process and the rationale when having these discussions.

Policy Makers

The importance of connecting with policy makers in the first thirty days and throughout the interim period differs significantly, depending upon the position's normal engagement with legislators or other government officials. As with the director of development, an early meeting with the director of government affairs is critical in the front end or, at a minimum, the first thirty days.

Obviously, influential state and federal legislators are critical connections for interim presidents of public universities. In these cases, the engagement strategy will depend on several critical factors, such as whether the legislature is in session, whether the university has any key legislative initiatives in motion, and the university's past level of engagement with lawmakers. Legislators do not like to be surprised by their constituents and want to feel valued, so reaching out to key allies in state and federal government is a high priority. There will likely be a short list of officials who should be contacted in week one. Work with the director of government affairs to develop a list of key government officials and any vital points to discuss during these high-priority contacts.

Interim presidents should work with their government affairs staff to prioritize contacts with policy makers. The importance of these contacts depends on a number of factors, including the institution's legislative agenda, the amount of time before the next legislative session, and the level of the predecessor's engagement with policy makers.

When I assumed the role of interim president, we had just gained authorization from the state legislature to start a medical school. This authorization had been accompanied by funding for the first year of the project only, so it was critical to get in front of key legislators and instill in them the confidence that we could deliver on our commitment and the aggressive timeline that my predecessor had negotiated.

During my first three months in the interim position, the legislative relations staff and I made over forty face-to-face visits with influential state legislators. Our message was simple; we will deliver on the medical school commitment, and we will regularly provide you with progress updates. Making these contacts in person was critical, as we needed to quickly gain the trust and confidence of the legislators. We named the medical school after the deceased former president to honor his vision and commitment, so the name also served to remind everyone of our resolve. The medical school went from legislative approval to having in place a first class of medical students within eighteen months, and funding was received in quarterly increments over the next four years.

For interim deans, vice presidents, and provosts, there may be a small number of public officials who should be touched. For interim deans, these officials are typically responsible for agencies with whom the college has established relationships. For example, an interim dean of agriculture described introductory meetings with the heads of state agencies responsible for agriculture and the environment. An interim dean of education reached out to the leader of the state department of education, whose agency relied heavily on the college for policy advice and continuing education needs. Included in this group of public officials are leaders of accreditation organizations.

Chapter 9

MANAGING YOUR WORK LIFE AND YOURSELF

Interim leadership positions can be stressful, time-consuming, and energy draining. It is important to establish control over many of the potentially detrimental effects of assuming the new role. Managing your personal life and health are critical to professional success. The organization needs you in top form, so maintaining a high level of physical, emotional, and mental health is a priority. Taking care of your health, maintaining a support network, retaining proper work/life balance, and having a healthy relationship with your boss are all keys to success.

TAKING CARE OF YOURSELF

It is tempting for interim leaders to ignore or downplay the emotional costs of their new role. Periods of leadership transition can be uncertain times, and interims often feel pressure to attend to others' needs and ignore their own. The weight on the shoulders of interim leaders, particularly those who assume the role in times of turmoil, can be enormous. Survival and success in an interim executive leadership position require strategies for maintaining the health and vitality essential to sustaining your efforts.

Work/Life Balance

Maintaining proper work/life balance is an essential survival skill for an executive leader. Much has been written about work/life balance; setting aside an appropriate amount of time and energy for family, friends, spiritual life, recreation, and so on is an important goal for any executive leader. You cannot outwork the job, and allocation of time to meaningful activities outside of work should be a conscious priority during the period of the interim appointment.

It is important to understand that complete separation of work life and personal life is not a precondition for maintaining work/life balance. Your personal life and your university life are not mutually exclusive activities. To illustrate, in the simple Venn diagram in Figure 9.1, the two circles represent your personal and university lives—that is to say, the degree to which your persona is broadly defined by each. The intersection of the two represents the areas where the nature of your work bears any relation to things that interest you in your spare time. Those with little overlap (top diagram) tend to lead separate home and work lives, a situation that can lead to frustration or conflict. People with more overlap (bottom diagram) can find themselves better reconciled and derive utility from activities that fall into both circles.

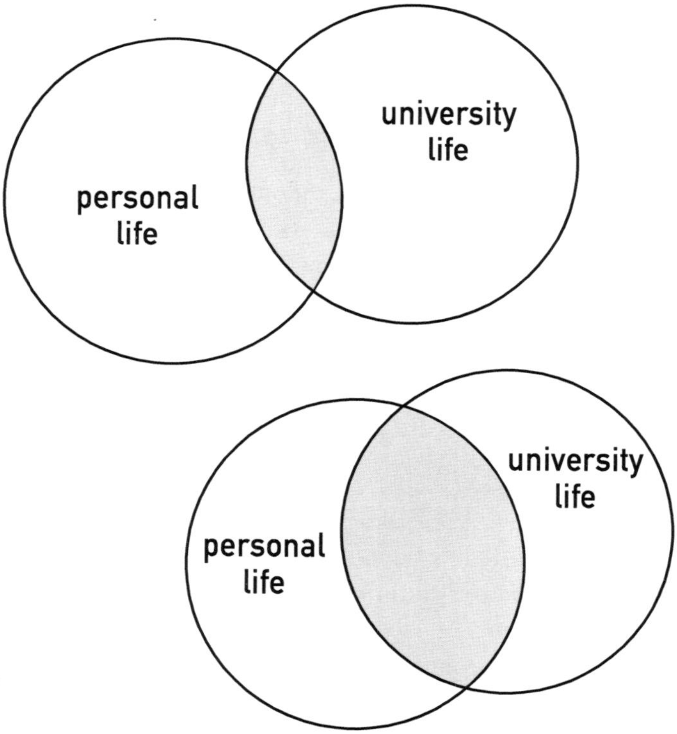

Figure 9.1. Work/Life Balance Diagram

It is noteworthy that as one climbs up the administrative ladder in university leadership, these circles tend to converge. The ultimate convergence is demonstrated by the life of a college or university president whose time outside of traditional work hours is often dedicated to social events, fundraising, athletic events, travel, and so on. Often, the partner is also engaged in this work. This factor does not imply that university presidents need not reserve time and energy for personal pursuits. They certainly do. But it does propose that those who derive both personal pleasure and utility and work benefit from these activities are likely going to feel more reconciled and fulfilled.

Time and Stress Management

Just about every interim leader interviewed mentioned taking care of oneself as an important lesson learned. Several interim leaders were not prepared for the stress that came with their new position. In fact, some experienced stress levels that translated into significant health issues during and/or after their appointment. It is difficult to prepare yourself for this type of stress, but proactively engaging in stress-relieving activities is highly recommended.

Heightened stress is probably inevitable when taking on a challenging new executive position. Not all stress is a bad thing; in fact, there is a well-documented relationship between stress and job performance (Figure 9.2). Small levels of stress, perhaps in the form of positive incentives or deadlines, keep us productive and engaged. As stress is increased, performance actually improves; however, you eventually reach a point where stress levels start adversely impacting performance. This dynamic creates more stress, further reducing performance, and eventually leading to burnout. The key is to manage the job and yourself to stay in the optimum range. Several of the interim leaders interviewed definitely went beyond safe stress levels and began sliding in their performance. Fortunately, most were able to curb the downward spiral by learning the job, getting help, and employing some coping skills.

STRESS CURVE

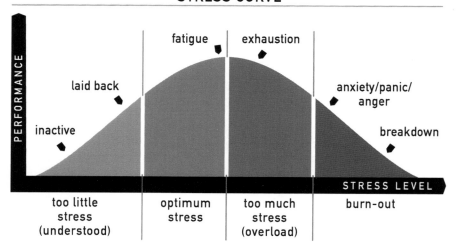

Figure 9.2. Yerkes-Dodson Human Performance Curve. Adapted from Godin, K. and Hansen, J. "Physical task stress and speaker variability in voice quality." *EURASIP Journal on Audio Speech and Music Processing*. October 2015.

In an earlier case presented in chapter 1, Claire, an interim dean, replaced another interim dean who had only served in the position for two weeks before he died. After the first interim dean did not appear at the dean's funeral, he was found dead in his home, having suffered a massive heart attack. This is a gut-wrenching story, and no one will ever know whether the heart attack was caused by the sudden stress imposed on the new dean who had no previous medical history. However, the story does serve as a grim reminder of life's frailty and how important it is to keep our professional lives in perspective while making our own health a top priority.

Just about every leader indicated that they were not prepared for the time demands of their new position. Any job requires more hours during the initial year than subsequent years. The challenge with higher education positions is that many activities run on a one-year cycle, so an interim executive rarely gets to realize the benefit of replication efficiencies. Every activity in the position's annual cycle—e.g., budget development, annual reviews, legislative sessions—is encountered for the first time. A trusted and competent support staff provides great value in helping to handle these activities.

Most interim leaders surveyed responded to this challenge by trying to outwork the job—several through working sixty to seventy hours a week. This schedule does not allow for stress-reducing activities and adequate detachment from the job and can place the interim leader in a downward spiral. Several approaches to reduce this time demand were discussed in chapter 4. Most importantly, one must develop the discipline to schedule blocks of work time during business hours, so that nights and weekends are not entirely consumed by catching up on paperwork, emails, and correspondence.

There are many opportunities for the interim leader to maintain physical, emotional, and mental health. Here are some essential steps:

- **Take proactive measures to advance personal health.**
  Obviously, there are many commonsense strategies such as diet, exercise, sleep, and relaxation that will assist leaders in maintaining their own personal health. Several interim leaders interviewed noted that they brought healthy habits into the position, only to have the new time demands and stress levels throw them off their daily rhythm. Mustering the discipline to maintain healthy routines is a laudable goal.

- **Delegate.**
  If there is one skill that should be mastered by all executive leaders, it's delegation. This is particularly true for interim leaders, because they have neither the time nor the expertise to delve into others' responsibilities. Not only will delegation give you more "brain space" and time to devote to priority issues, but it will also empower your team. Some additional insights around delegation are provided in chapter 5.

- **Prioritize.**
  As explained in chapter 4, the art of prioritization is a crucial survival skill for the interim leader. An ability to quickly assess the organization's issues and activities and prioritize them is a critical step in avoiding

sixty- to seventy-hour workweeks and the baneful effects that accompany them.

- **Stay positive.**
Executive leader roles are by their nature heavily and visibly symbolic. Therefore, it is critical that your actions and words communicate a positive and confident direction. Staying positive is critical if you are fortunate enough to inherit a positive culture and perhaps even more important if you are trying to move the culture to a positive place. Avoid criticizing past leadership. Maintaining a positive attitude also contributes to your own mental health.

- **Know your personal and professional boundaries.**
An important survival skill is the ability to realize the distinction between yourself and your work role. As a leader, you must recognize that others react to you largely in response to the role they occupy rather than as individuals. Negative reactions are often transferences or projections from distressed or disappointed others. This can be very difficult for new leaders who have not had much experience with such behavior in previous roles. Most difficult decisions will generate disappointment, perhaps even anger, in some colleagues, and the frequency of these necessarily difficult decisions increases as one's position rises in the university hierarchy.

Constituents often personalize their reaction to a decision they do not like. You might have acquired a Teflon coat from previous positions and life experiences; if not, you will need to build one quickly. This does not mean that a leader is insensitive to the needs and feelings of others; it means that when attacks become personal, the leader does not internalize them or return fire. This skill allows leaders to make and live with difficult decisions.

- **Know what is and what is not your business.**
As a new leader, part of prioritizing is knowing the boundaries of your position and the organization you are learning. There will likely be many people trying to command your attention and reaction to issues that are not within your domain. In supervising several interim leaders, I have encountered instances where the leader brought for-

ward a difficult issue, to which I rightly responded, "That is not your problem." They left my office feeling relieved that a major problem was just lifted from their shoulders. There are plenty of issues to address without taking on others' problems.

- **Continue to invest in learning.**
  As the saying goes, "What got you here won't get you there." All of us in higher education believe in learning, but administrators sometimes become so busy and overcommitted that they ignore this aspect of their professional life. "I'll do that later" leads to long-term stagnation in personal and professional growth.

Maximize the professional development aspects of this opportunity. It may be a more enduring value of the experience than any legacy you leave with the organization or unit. It takes enormous discipline (and maybe a little selfishness) to accomplish this end. If you can muster the discipline, it is worth keeping a daily journal of some of the key issues and events that occur during the interim period. This will come in particularly handy if you choose to apply for similar positions in the future.

DEVELOPING A SUPPORTIVE NETWORK

Executive leadership can be a lonely job, and research has shown that successful leaders develop and utilize effective support networks. Such a network can be helpful in a variety of ways, including serving as a sounding board for ideas, offering nonjudgmental feedback, providing helpful suggestions, and increasing accountability—i.e., serving as a reminder of your personal values, institutional mission, and past commitments or promises.

A support network may take a variety of forms; it can be comprised of personal relationships outside of work, colleagues within the institution, and professionals from outside the institution. One can naturally gravitate toward like-minded colleagues when forming a support network; however, it is important to include a diversity of backgrounds and perspectives in your network. Earlier, the concept of addressing your "blind spots" was introduced. Having people in your support system who can help identify and address these "blind spots" can be extremely helpful. Make certain to include some advisers who are from underrepresented communities, as their observations and perspectives can be extremely helpful.

Do not be too restrictive in seeking out your support network. Leaning on friends with no relationship to professional life can provide a needed separation from the workplace. Personally, I found business and industry leaders that I had befriended over my university career to be some of the most helpful mentors and confidants. They tended to approach issues and problems a little differently than most academics and, hence, provided a very useful and alternative perspective.

Each member of your support network may have a unique role. As a starting point, Watkins (2013) proposes three types of advisers for the professional dimension of your life:

- **Technical advisers** provide expert analysis of technologies, programs, and strategy.

- **Cultural interpreters** help you understand the culture of the new organization and adapt to it.

- **Political counselors** help you address political relationships and power dynamics within the new organization and with other units across the institution.

Broad support, incorporating at least one person from each group, is a consideration as you build your support network.

Personal relationships were cited by most interim leaders interviewed as important in managing the stress of the position. As noted earlier, executive leadership positions can be lonely jobs, and not surprisingly, interims interviewed frequently cited the support they received from home as an important source of inspiration and comfort. A supportive partner can provide a sympathetic ear and, in positions such as interim president, will likely be needed to help with some of the position's external responsibilities.

WORKING WITH YOUR BOSS

There's an old saying that states, "Everyone has a boss." For the provost and vice president, it's the president; for deans, it is typically the provost; and for the president or chancellor, it's usually the institution's governing board—e.g., board of trustees, board of regents. Maintaining a healthy and productive relationship with your boss is key to successful interim leadership.

Leadership is often equated with managing the people who report to you, but savvy academic administrators understand that leading up is every bit as important. In the culture of the academy, where resources are scarce and relationships are vital for opening doors, the ability to understand, influence, and work closely with your boss and other senior players is one of the most important tasks in administrative work. Despite what cynics might think, "managing up" does not equate with self-serving manipulation. It is instead a strategic approach for developing clear expectations and communication patterns that enable you and your supervisor to work productively together.

Fostering a Healthy Relationship with Your Boss

A relationship with your superior carries a special twist because of the inherent power differential. In the face of power differences, Gabarro and Kotter (2008) advise understanding and avoiding two common reactions to authority. On one side of the spectrum is overdependence—responding to a boss in a fearful or overly compliant manner. On the other side is counter-dependence—resistance to being controlled, which often leads subordinates to reject, resent, or battle authority. The key to a healthy relationship with your boss is to find the sweet spot along this continuum.

Most bosses are extremely supportive of the interim leaders they have asked to serve. They fully understand the imposition this request places on interim leaders and appreciate their willingness to serve for the good of the organization. Of course, let's be honest, not all executives are compassionate and competent; there is a remote chance that the relationship with the boss could bring an added challenge to the interim appointment. In such cases, it is up to the interim to work on bringing the relationship to a stronger and more productive footing (Dobson and Dobson 2002).

Three overarching goals for the superior-subordinate relationship are partnership, open communication, and credibility (Carlone and Hill 2008).

- **Partnership**
  A partnership is a cooperative venture with mutual objectives, and the superior-subordinate relationship should be viewed as such. Building partnership requires conversation and shared agreement about roles,

expectations, and assessment standards. As noted in chapter 1, this partnership is initiated prior to accepting the job.

- **Communication**
  The ideal time to begin this conversation is before you accept the job, but it is never too late to start. The goal is to clarify what each of you needs from the other. You need things like information, direction, counsel, support, and resources from your boss. Your boss needs stable leadership, advancement toward the organization's primary goals, and a smooth transition to the permanent leader. Regular and constructive communication is needed throughout the interim period.

- **Credibility**
  Credibility is needed to negotiate key work priorities with superiors and gain their support and trust in implementing change. Credibility is built upon communication.

Keys to Productive Relationships with Superiors

Here are some key elements for interim deans, vice presidents, or provosts to employ in establishing productive working relationships with their superiors:

- **First, understand the boss.**
  Each provost and president has a unique administrative style. It's up to the interim to conform to the boss's way of doing business. Like the interim, the boss also has a unique set of problems, pressures, and priorities. It is critical to understand these. Find out how the boss likes to communicate so that you can provide information in a form that works (Kotter 1985).

- **Find the right balance between keeping the boss informed and operating with the appropriate level of independence.**
  Presidents and provosts do not like to be blindsided, so it is best to keep them informed. However, most leaders do not want to be besieged with tactical questions and logistical issues, so avoid overwhelming them with these details. Finding this balance will require some trial and error as executives have differing preferences about how much they want to know. Some areas where you want to keep your boss informed are major personnel moves (particularly terminations), serious workplace

environment issues, decisions they might hear about from their superior, and things that might show up in the press.

- **Provide solutions, not problems.**
  Instead of presenting a problem, try, "Here's what I see, here's what I've done, here's what I've learned, and here's my plan" (Kotter 1985).

- **Manage expectations.**
  Bosses don't like surprises. If something is taking a turn for the worse, let your superior know there's a problem and that you have a plan for how to solve it. These strategies will help your boss get up to speed and realize you are reliable.

- **Speak up when necessary.**
  Some interims are reluctant to speak up in meetings or when they disagree with the boss. This reticence compromises credibility and effectiveness.

For presidents, the relationship with one's boss is a little different, as it normally involves a governing board. None of the interim presidents interviewed encountered any significant issues with their board. Boards were generally very supportive. Most interim presidents interviewed had a prior relationship with the board from their previous position, and this provided a head start in developing mutual trust and respect.

Interim presidents discussed the balancing act between managing the politics of the position and making positive change within the organization they inherited. This issue is particularly relevant for interims interested in filling their position on a permanent basis. On one hand, many people, including board members, scrutinize the interim's performance to assess their effectiveness in managing change. On the other hand, one must be cognizant of the ramifications of implementing changes that may be politically unpopular.

Who Has Your Back?

The number one piece of advice from interim deans, vice presidents, and provosts was this: make certain that the boss has your back. Without exception, someone in their organization challenged their decisions and went around them to the next level of administration. The unequivocal support of one's superior is requisite for the success of an interim leader. Nothing can shut down an interim leader's effectiveness quicker than someone successfully pulling off an "end around" with the next level of authority.

A case in chapter 5 reflected on a situation where the interim dean, Tim, was appointed into a "clean up the mess" interim role that required him to ratchet up the accountability of the leadership team. Unit leaders were not being held accountable to their annual budgets, and the college was in financial disarray. Unit leaders and some senior faculty professed to have several verbal deals with the former dean that, if honored, would have put the college deeper in debt. Further investigation revealed that many of these alleged commitments were not documented, or else the available documentation did not reflect a hard and fast commitment. When Tim chose not to honor some of these alleged commitments, several unit leaders and faculty went directly to the provost. The provost steadfastly defended Tim's actions, and he cited this response as the most important factor in establishing his authority and credibility in the effort to rectify the college's dire budgetary outlook.

Of course, all executives who appoint an interim leader will profess to have the interim's back; but the truth is, that is not always the case. A couple of interim leaders interviewed described situations where, when the politics escalated, their superior did not back them up.

In your initial meetings, establish up front what you expect from your boss. Be as specific as possible. If there are certain decisions that you believe might generate pushback from faculty or staff, define the issues and potential responses clearly and gain a commitment that you will be supported. Such assurances are difficult to abrogate.

TURNING THE INTERIM ROLE INTO A PERMANENT POSITION

About half of interim leaders interviewed entered their role with no interest in assuming the position permanently. Those who were interested in the permanent position cited the importance of accomplishment during the interim period. The period was viewed as a time to showcase their abilities to their superiors, the entire team, and individuals throughout the organization. Those who were successful in securing the permanent position identified two critical aspects of their leadership that were particularly important to their success: first, an unwavering commitment to critical values such as fairness, respect, integrity, and inclusion; second, a demonstrated ability to lead with an action imperative and achieve desired outcomes.

They also cited the need to balance accomplishment with minimizing politically unpopular decisions. This balance is probably the trickiest aspect of leading in an interim role with the objective of securing the permanent position. Obviously, if there are behavioral issues that compromise the workplace climate, those must be addressed despite any potential political consequences. In fact, addressing those is a sure-fire way of demonstrating your commitment to values important to you and your colleagues. Most significant changes will yield some discontent, so managing any pushback with good communications and demonstrating value to the organization is critical. Avoid "sacred cows." They can be addressed when you have the permanent position.

Clearly, establishing a productive relationship with your supervisor is paramount in maximizing your chances for obtaining the permanent position. Keeping him/her in close alignment when tackling potentially controversial changes will mitigate adverse consequences of implementing changes and allow you to demonstrate your talent in leading with an action imperative.

One must be prepared for the possibility of not obtaining the permanent position (Shellenbarger 2016). Being passed over after competing for the permanent position can be difficult for one's ego. Higher education, as opposed to business and industry, seems to have an inherent bias toward going outside the institution when hiring executive leaders. The governing board and/or search committee may be compelled to select the bright, shiny object (newcomer from the outside) as opposed to the well-worn and maybe slightly tarnished one that has served in the interim role. Interviewees who were not selected for the permanent position universally expressed that difficulties returning to the former position were more challenging than anticipated.

It is important to stay positive and not criticize your successor. Find out why you were not selected without challenging the decision. Then determine whether there is a place for you in the institution or you should apply elsewhere.

Chapter 10

THE HANDOFF

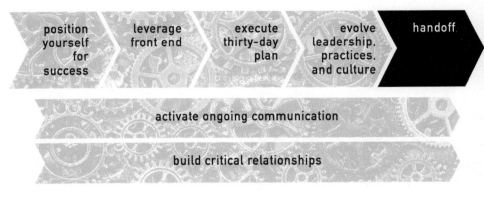

Figure 10.1. Interim Leadership Timeline, Stage 5: The Handoff

You are heading down the homestretch. A new permanent leader has been identified, and a starting date has been announced. Creating a smooth transition for your successor has been a priority throughout your interim service; thus, a successful handoff has been top-of-mind throughout. Nonetheless, the handoff period starts in earnest when your successor is formally announced.

Navigating the handoff involves four primary activities: first, working with your team to prepare the organization for the new leader; second, working with the incoming leader to provide whatever information and resources he or she finds helpful in easing the transition; third, providing key deliverables to the successor; and finally, transitioning yourself to your former position or an alternative role.

PREPARING FOR THE NEW EXECUTIVE LEADER

Typically, the search process for a permanent leader will be occurring for the lion's share of the interim executive leader's appointment. This activity can be somewhat distracting, but it is important not to let it take the organization off course. The pivotal turning point is when the search is completed and the new permanent leader is announced. There is little doubt that the interim leader's role transforms into a different status at this point. This does not have to be a lame-duck status, but people will perceive the interim leader as truly temporary once a permanent leader and a starting date are made known. At the same time, this is a crucial period to push through some key projects and activities to cap your service and prepare a smooth glide path for your successor.

Throughout the book, we have stressed the important goal of setting your successor up for success. In the cases provided, several scenarios were reported where the interim took on issues to provide the incoming leader with a strong starting point. If an interim executive implements many of the actions proposed here, this end will have largely been accomplished.

Preparation for the new leader takes many forms. First and most important is a well-functioning organization with a winning attitude and culture. This includes a highly motivated leadership team and functional areas such as budget and finance, communications, and development.

A second preparation step is that all normal administrative processes and projects are current and moving forward. This includes such things as annual budgeting, annual performance reviews, and so on. Something that can stymie the initial progress of an incoming leader is the presence of a large number of unreconciled issues that are urgent and unimportant. Taking care of as many of these as possible will provide more time for the incoming leader to focus on strategic issues.

A third vital step is documentation. Documentation takes on two forms: (1) normal documentation that should be in place for any organization to function well and continue operations in the event of the departure of key personnel, and (2) transition documents that are explicitly developed for the incoming leader. The development of transition documents is an important activity for the final couple months of the interim's appointment. To guide the preparation of these materials, remember what you went through to assimilate information. What was helpful? What was not? Ask the incoming leader what would be helpful for you and the team to prepare.

Make yourself available to the incoming leader. It is a reasonable expectation that incoming leaders provide some direction to outgoing interim leaders about what, when, and how they will be briefed. My personal approach as an outgoing interim was to keep the interactions very factual and not offer opinions unless they were specifically requested. I found it helpful to work with the leadership team to prepare some initial written materials for the incoming executive and use those to frame initial discussions and let them determine where to take the conversations.

Interim leaders interviewed had very different interactions with the incoming leader. The majority were embraced by their successor and had very substantive conversations about the organization's inner workings. However, surprisingly, several did not. In these cases, the new leader was not particularly interested in the interim's perspective and did not engage at a substantive level.

An interesting issue is whether incoming leaders should ask their predecessors about key personnel and any personnel issues they have encountered. Some incoming leaders desire to give everyone a fresh start and don't want to taint their interactions with the former leader's perspectives. Personally, I always wanted to glean as much information as I could from my predecessors. Their perspectives were simply part of the information assimilation process and among the many sources I used to develop an assessment of team members.

DELIVERABLES TO YOUR SUCCESSOR

Throughout the book, suggestions were provided of various assets you can present to the incoming executive leader. For ease of reference, let's inventory those suggestions, which are grouped into the three aforementioned categories: (1) documentation, (2) a well-functioning organization, and (3) projects and activities.

Solid Documentation

- **Glossary of terms and acronyms (chapter 2)**
  Incoming leaders will likely be overwhelmed by organizational lingo. A highly useful resource, particularly for those coming from outside the institution, is a glossary of terms, acronyms, and abbreviations.

- **Documentation of any commitments (chapter 5)**
  Unwinding past commitments that were not codified can be a difficult and time-consuming task for an interim. Don't leave any of these for your successor to deal with.

- **Up-to-date position descriptions and annual reviews (chapter 5)**
  Ideally, you inherited current personnel documentation. If not, an important task was updating position descriptions and completing annual performance reviews for the interim period. These documents will provide a great starting point for the new leader and an opportunity to check in with employees on their progress toward objectives for the period of interim leadership and accomplishments.

- **Annual budgets (chapter 7)**
  No institution should be without an annual operating budget for the organization and each of its units. In addition, budget processes should be in place for unit leaders to be held accountable to their budgets.

- **Financial statements (chapter 7)**
  The incoming leader will benefit greatly from accurate reports on the organization's financial health. These financials should reflect current account balances as well as encumbrances on accounts.

Organizational Elements

- **Well-functioning leadership team (chapters 2 through 8)**
  As noted throughout this book, the presence of a well-functioning leadership team characterized by a common mission, a commitment to excellence, and a culture of accountability is the greatest gift the interim leader can provide to the successor.

- **Identified land mines (chapter 2)**
  The interim period likely involved identifying and navigating around land mines within the organization. By sharing these discoveries with

their successors, interims allow them to avoid these issues, which might otherwise short-circuit their early leadership.

- **Competent support staff (chapter 4)**
  One of the most helpful resources for a new leader is an empowered and confident support staff. These positions include the executive assistant as well as those who direct functional areas such as budget and finance, communications, and development.

- **Minimal carryover personnel issues (chapter 5)**
  Unaddressed personnel problems can be a hindrance for new executive leaders. Oftentimes it is not possible to fully address these issues within the interim period, but taking positive steps to rectify them, providing the necessary communications to the offending parties, and documenting the history are all helpful.

- **Cued-up searches, if appropriate (chapter 5)**
  A useful strategy for some essential positions that come open is to initiate a search that culminates after the new leader is on board. This approach allows the new executive to select the team member and shortens the time the organization is without the critical position.

- **Successful new hires (if appropriate) who are well-onboarded (chapter 5)**
  If it was essential to hire new team members during the interim period, these new employees should be well-mentored and assimilated into the organization.

- **A functional organizational structure (chapter 6)**
  The new leader will ultimately decide on the appropriate organizational structure, but the interim should make structural changes to address fundamental structural problems. These changes will provide the incoming leader with a good place to start.

Projects and Activities

- **Completed projects (chapter 3)**
  The action plan included several projects to complete or advance during the interim period, including those ongoing when the interim stepped in, those identified by the supervisor, and those identified by

the interim and the interim's team. A successful period of service is concluded with these projects completed or tracking to completion.

- **Early wins (chapter 3)**
  Every incoming leader needs early wins. Ideally, there are some projects or activities that the successor can deliver on during the early phases of his or her appointment.

- **Up-to-date administrative processes (chapter 6)**
  Academic units engage in many administrative processes, typically on an annual cycle. A backlog of incomplete processes can frustrate an incoming leader.

- **Teed-up gifts from development activities (chapter 8)**
  A common development strategy for the interim period is to build a bundle of unannounced gifts, pledges, and teed-up gifts. Optimally, the new permanent leader will be able roll out pieces of this bundle during his or her initial months in office, thus establishing credibility and success.

TRANSITIONING BACK TO YOUR FORMER ROLE

Interviews of former interim executives revealed that transitioning back to one's former position was one of the most challenging aspects of interim service. The smoothness of this transition is greatly influenced by the work of the supervisor and interim leader prior to starting the position. Ideally, terms for returning to the former position or another role were clearly discussed and described in the letter of appointment.

As noted in chapter 1, specific terms and conditions for returning to the former position can take a variety of forms. A sabbatical leave can be very helpful for outgoing interim executives as a chance to catch their breath and/or retool before returning to their former position. This is a particularly helpful strategy for interim deans who may be returning to a faculty role with research and teaching responsibilities. Some former interim deans interviewed negotiated a resource package for restarting their research program. People serving in interim roles are more experienced and skilled administrators following their service, so they may be able to negotiate for increased responsibilities and an expanded position description relative to their previous role. Finally, additional compensation is often delivered that reflects service provided to the institution.

For some interim leaders, the return to their previous role can be very difficult, particularly if they have returned to a position within the organization they were leading. It can be uncomfortable because, instead of leading, you are once again following. This may upset your routine and make you feel less valued. In addition, peers who became subordinates are now peers again. Sometimes, peers can hold grudges based on decisions made during a person's time as interim leader. On the positive side, you will likely experience new and deeper relationships with executive leaders, external stakeholders, and so on.

Essentially, all the above steps for transitioning new leaders into an organization apply in one form or another to interims returning to their former roles. Ideally, the person who filled your position as an interim will provide many of the deliverables you have left for your successor. The interim leader can serve as a great resource to get you back on course quickly and up to speed on key issues, opportunities, and activities.

Recognition for the interim leader and the team that held everything together in your absence is an important step in returning to your former role. Remember, the outgoing interim leader is going through some of the same feelings and challenges you may be experiencing as a result of leaving your recent role.

It is also important to realize that not all interim leaders intending to return to their previous position actually go back to their former role. Sometimes circumstances change in their former organization, and their former role may not be as attractive as it once was. Other times, their outstanding work is recognized by upper management and they are asked to take on new administrative opportunities.

Final Thoughts

Interim leadership has become more prevalent in higher education as turnover in executive positions has accelerated in recent years. Contributing to this situation is a lack of succession planning and poor leadership development activities at most colleges and universities. While interim leaders are sometimes viewed as placeholders until a permanent leader arrives, that mindset needs to change, and interim leaders need to lead with a bias toward action.

What are the key takeaways from this assessment of the state of interim leadership in higher education? From my personal experience, the experiences of those interviewed who had previously served in interim roles, and reviewing research on the topic, a few general conclusions can be reached. First, successful interim leaders come from different backgrounds and employ a variety of leadership styles. Regardless of leadership style, some useful qualities for the interim leader are administrative experience, selflessness, excellent communication and collaboration skills, and good administrative instincts. Given their varied backgrounds and the myriad of scenarios they may walk into, there is no magic formula for leaders successfully navigating these positions. A critical capability for interim executives is being able to quickly assess a situation and adapt to move the organization in the right direction.

Personally, I found each of my interim appointments to be a positive experience; and without exception, everyone interviewed considered it a productive use of their time. Universally, the most rewarding aspect of the opportunity for former interim leaders was the positive impact they felt they had on the organization. The challenge of pulling together as a team and working together to transition the organization was professionally fulfilling.

When asked about their greatest accomplishment, most former interim leaders did not point to a tangible product, such as a new program or facility. Instead, they focused on organizational improvement such as fixing dysfunctional internal processes, improving the work environment, or getting the unit's finances in order. Even though several appointments lasted longer than a year, these leaders found that the time went quickly and wished they had more time to effect change.

From a professional development perspective, the interim position was certainly a worthwhile experience, particularly for those with aspirations of advancing up the administrative ranks. The opportunity provided experience and visibility that led to an upward move. Several interims interviewed successfully competed for the permanent position. Others were successful locating a similar position at another institution. After experiencing the job, some learned that they did not want to pursue that type of position in the future. This is an important outcome that can save someone from an ill-fated career move and institutions from hiring leaders who will likely not stay in the position very long.

Not surprisingly, a key to success for many interim leaders was preparation. Most importantly, those best prepared had directly relevant prior leadership experience. Those who participated in formal leadership development programs viewed these experiences as helpful preparation. Finally, those who leveraged the time between their appointment and the first day on the job were better prepared to hit the ground running.

Several of the leaders interviewed were surprised with the difficulty of their interim positions. While they generally felt prepared for the various administrative responsibilities—e.g., budget, program management—or were able to climb the learning curve necessary to lead in those areas, they were not prepared for the size and scope of the responsibilities. For these individuals, the position had a much larger impact on their lives than anticipated, largely due to time demands and stress.

The primary source of stress to interims came from personal interactions with team members and complex personnel actions. Interim leaders encounter a myriad of responses from team members, ranging from high levels of cooperation to outward resistance. A proactive response to uncooperative team members was identified as a critical action by several of the interviewees. While most had prior experience with personnel management, the number and complexity of the personnel situations encountered in their new position was greater and presented new administrative challenges. Building up the necessary Teflon needed to avoid personalizing these interactions was an important survival skill.

Many of the difficulties experienced by interim leaders emanated from challenging circumstances within the organizations they were charged to lead. The demanding environment facing higher education over the past decade has posed challenges for everyone in leadership roles, and interims are likely even more vulnerable than their permanent counterparts. Interims interviewed dealt with a much greater level of organizational dysfunction than expected. Sometimes the need for an interim leader results from the position being vacated when the previous leader proved ineffective or stepped down because the position was too frustrating or stressful. Therefore, it is not atypical for an interim leader to walk into an inflamed situation.

While they found taking on an interim position a generally worthwhile experience, interviewees did reveal a few frequent negative outcomes. First, some experienced difficulty returning to their previous position with perhaps less authority and prestige. This feeling is not about losing power. Most people who successfully serve in leadership roles find the work meaningful and rewarding, and not having that impact can create a void in their professional life. For those who applied for the permanent role and did not receive an offer, a return to their previous position was particularly difficult and often resulted in the person leaving the institution. For faculty who stepped into an interim role, an often-cited concern was the adverse impact on scholarly activities. Getting a research program back up and running after a one-year or longer hiatus is not an easy task.

There was not much unanimity among previous interim leaders in terms of mistakes or misgivings. In looking back, some interim leaders wished they had gone into the position with a more well-thought-out plan of action but corrected this mistake by creating one "on the fly" during the first couple months. Some recognized that they may have moved too fast in making significant changes and encountered unexpected resistance. On the other hand, some wished that they had moved faster on personnel issues identified early on, as the problems continued to fester and became even more disruptive and difficult to address.

There is a plethora of advice and recommendations throughout this book to aid you in navigating the trials and tribulations of an interim leadership role. To assist you in locating this information, a "Quick Help Guide" is included, which provides page numbers for easy reference on a given topic.

Perhaps the most important piece of advice I can offer someone taking on an interim leadership role is to make the most of your time in the position. Enjoy this unique opportunity. These positions can be extremely rewarding and important to the long-term success of the organization. They are particularly well suited for people who enjoy a new challenge—they will test your administrative mettle. You will be required to respond to situations you have not encountered in the past, in a shorter time frame, without having as much background knowledge as you are accustomed to. For those aspiring to higher administration positions, there is no better preparation than taking on an interim role. For those without these aspirations, there are few more meaningful ways to serve your organization and colleagues.

Quick Help Guide

Administrative Processes—Before handing the position off to your successor, assure that all normal administrative processes and projects are current and moving forward. (Chapter 10) 152

Advice—Seek advice from those who have been through similar circumstances. (Chapter 2) 30

Announcing Your Appointment—When announcing your appointment, make certain your superior includes a timeline and the process to be employed for moving to permanent leadership. (Chapter 2) 34

Blocks of Time—Carve out and protect blocks of time in your initial months to provide periods to analyze the situation and develop plans. (Chapter 4) 53

Budget Review—When reviewing budgets, assure that allocations align with mission and strategy. (Chapter 7) 103

Clear Breakpoint—Leave your previous position behind; establish a clear breakpoint when you are out of your former position (mentally and physically) and into the new interim role. (Chapter 2) 33

Communication—Communicate up and down the organization, and within and outside the organization. (Chapter 3) 41

Control of Your Time—The first step in gaining control of your time is to develop a thorough understanding of where your time is spent. (Chapter 4) 53

Culture—Don't underestimate the influence of culture on the success of your term as an interim leader. Conduct a BRAVE culture assessment of the organization. (Chapter 1) 3

Deliverables—Define deliverables (outcomes) for the period of interim service up front and keep them top-of-mind. (Chapter 3) 36

Development—Allocating time, energy, and thought to development requires discipline. Carve out a specific number of days each month to dedicate to development and other external activities. (Chapter 8) 124

Development Prospects—Complete an inventory of all key development prospects. (Chapter 8) 126

Discrimination—As you assess individual team members, be on the lookout for situations where individuals may not have been supported by supervisors or fellow team members or have been victims of discrimination. (Chapter 5) 77

Diversity, Equity, and Inclusion—As part of your early assessment activities, identify past efforts to advance these policies and identify whether a plan exists for the unit. (Chapter 3) 75

Documentation—Don't invite new team members to send you documentation unless you provide some ground rules. Control the flow of information by asking for specific documents and formats. (Chapter 2) 30

Due Diligence—Perform your due diligence before accepting a position by collecting information from a variety of sources to evaluate the opportunity and determine its fit with your skill set and administrative style. (Chapter 1) 3

Early Wins—Look for early wins to boost team morale and confidence in your leadership. (Chapter 3) 47

Executive Assistant—Make effective use of your executive assistant; he/she can be a tremendous resource in avoiding the allocation of time to minutia and staying focused on priorities. (Chapter 4) 57

External Stakeholders—Reach out to external stakeholders. Stakeholders should be prioritized for contact, with the highest priority receiving early and high-touch communication. (Chapter 8) 121

Finances—Understanding the organization's finances involves much more than digging into the numbers; spend time understanding the culture, history, policies, and practices employed in fiscal management. (Chapter 7) 104

Former Duties—Avoid the temptation (or a superior's request) to perform both your former duties as well as the new interim position. (Chapter 1) 9

Front End—Take advantage of the front end, the valuable time period between accepting a position and the first day on the job. (Chapter 2) 26

Go-to People—When assessing team members, be on the lookout for your go-to people and those you might be able to access to deliver on priorities. (Chapter 5) 73

Guiding Document—Work with your supervisor to develop a clear guiding document that defines key goals, critical outcomes, authority for making changes, and terms for returning to your former position. (Chapter 2) 23

Initial Meetings—When meeting your new leadership team, avoid the temptation to talk too much about your previous position. (Chapter 5) 67

Initial Message—Keep your initial message to the team simple and repeat it often. (Chapter 2) 30

Land Mines—Identify land mines as early as possible. (Chapter 2) 31

Launching Initiatives—Look for opportunities to "set the table" for your successor by launching needed initiatives that can provide him/her a head start in addressing a key issue. (Chapter 6) 95

Leadership Style—Be yourself and employ a leadership style that you are most comfortable with and that fits the situation. (Introduction) xviii

Leading Former Peers—If you move into a position where you are leading former peers, be certain to clearly define the new boundaries that define this new relationship. (Chapter 5) 71

Learning Plan—Develop a learning plan to assure that you are balancing learning with the other critical tasks of the position. (Chapter 3) 43

Letter of Appointment—Insist on a letter of appointment that clearly defines the position's roles and responsibilities, expectations, and the time frame for the interim position. (Chapter 2) 23

Listen, Hear, and Understand—Taking the time to listen, hear, and understand the people who make up the organization can help build rapport and credibility from the start. (Chapter 5) 66

Meetings—Review scheduled meetings and assess their value based upon duration, frequency, and having the right people in the room. (Chapter 4) 55

Messaging (to New Team)—If you are using it, dump the reluctant leader act and stop messaging that you really didn't want the job. It reduces your credibility and ability to lead. (Chapter 2) 31

Onboarding—Invest in onboarding activities. (Chapter 2) 31

Overlap (between current and interim roles)—If possible, provide some overlap between the outgoing leader and your presence in the new unit. (Chapter 2) 22

Personal Affairs—Get your personal affairs in order and your office setup in place before the first day of your new appointment. (Chapter 2) 33

Phasing Initial Communications—Phase initial communications so that messages build upon previous communications. (Chapter 3) 34

Political Repercussions—You can assist your successor significantly by taking on issues and making changes that may generate significant political repercussions. (Chapter 6) 95

Posteriorities—Not only set priorities, but also identify "posteriorities," deciding which tasks are not going to be tackled and sticking to the decision. (Chapter 4) 52

Preparation—Long before the opportunity presents itself, prepare for the interim leadership role by assuming various leadership roles, engaging in mentoring programs, and participating in leadership development activities. (Final Thoughts) 156

Prior Responsibilities—Shed as many of your prior responsibilities as possible before stepping into the interim role. (Chapter 4) 52

Priorities—Be clear about your most critical priorities in the short, medium, and longer term and identify the primary outcomes you want to achieve. (Chapter 4) 51

Prioritize Communications—It is vital to prioritize communications with stakeholders during the front end based on urgency and order of importance. (Chapter 2) 34

Professional Development—Consciously frame the position to maximize professional development benefits by writing down the goals you want to achieve from your service as an interim leader. (Chapter 1) 5

Relationships—Leadership works when relationships work; investing in these relationships may be the interim leader's most important early task. (Chapter 5) 64

Restructure—Do not be afraid to restructure if the current administrative structure is contributing to poor performance or dysfunction. (Chapter 6) 97

Returning to Your Former Position—Carefully and honestly consider how you will feel about returning to your former position and develop a plan for return. (Chapter 10) 152

Risk—Objectively assess the three primary sources of risk associated with taking on the interim position: personal risk, role risk, and organizational risk. (Chapter 1) 2

Schedule—Get control of your schedule. Do not accept your predecessor's schedule as one that is appropriate for your leadership. (Chapter 4) 52

Start Date—A subtle way of creating a little more preparation time is to extend the start date. If there's flexibility, which is not always the case, you might negotiate a longer front end. (Chapter 2) 27

Supervisor's Support—From the beginning, make sure that your boss has your back for the inevitable situation when someone challenges a decision and goes around you to the next level of authority. (Chapter 9) 143

Support Network—Develop a diverse support network that can provide emotional support and technical advice and serve as a useful sounding board. (Chapter 9) 139

Talking with New Team Members—When talking with new team members, steer the conversations to the present and future, stay positive, and listen more than you speak. (Chapter 5) 67

Team Building—Carve out time to invest in team building and individual relationship building activities. (Chapter 5) 65

Thirty-day Plan—An important activity prior to your first day is developing a thirty-day plan. (Chapter 3) 35

Thirty-day Plan Review—After completing your first month on the job, look back at the thirty-day plan to determine what you should stop, start, or continue doing to maximize team performance. (Chapter 3) 48

Time Frame (of appointment)—There should be an explicit time frame attached to the appointment. If there is not, insist upon it or at least upon a time when you and the supervisor will reevaluate continuation. (Chapter 1) 9

Transition Documents—In your final months, prepare a set of transition documents to help the new leader assimilate into the new position. (Chapter 10) 149

Transition Plan—Develop a clear transition plan and articulate it to all team members in a timely manner to reduce anxiety and prevent the rumor mill from starting to churn. (Chapter 2) 22

Transition from Former Unit—Take care of business in the unit you are leaving. It is your responsibility to develop a transition plan for your former unit and assure a smooth transfer of leadership. (Chapter 2) 27

References

Barr, M. J., and G. S. McClellan. 2010. *Budgets and Financial Management in Higher Education*. Hoboken: John Wiley and Sons, Inc.

BIE Executive. 2014. *A Guide to Interim Management*. BIE Executive Ltd. https://www.bie-executive.com/guides/guide-to-interim-management/.

Bichsel, Jacqueline, Adam Pritchard, Jingyun Li, and Jasper McChesney. 2018. "Administrators in Higher Education Annual Report: Key Findings, Trends, and Comprehensive Tables for the 2017-18 Academic Year" (Research Report). CUPA-HR. https://www.cupahr.org/wp-content/uploads/surveys/Results/2018-Administrators-Report-Overview.pdf.

Blodget, H. 2014. "LinkedIn's CEO Jeff Weiner Reveals the Importance of Body Language, Mistakes Made Out of Fear, and One Time He Really Doubted Himself." *Business Insider*. September 22, 2014. https://www.businessinsider.com/linkedin-ceo-jeff-weiner-on-leadership-2014-9.

Bolman, L. G., and J. V. Gallos. 2011. *Reframing Academic Leadership*. Hoboken: John Wiley and Sons, Inc.

Bradt, G. B. 2017. "What Follows a New Leader's 100-Day Action Plan?" *Forbes*, April 26, 2017. https://www.forbes.com/sites/georgebradt/2017/04/26/what-follows-a-new-leaders-100-day-action-plan/#a1d42451c23c.

Bradt, G. B., J. A. Check, and J. A. Lawler. 2016. *The New Leader's 100-Day Action Plan: How to Take Charge, Build or Merge Your Team, and Get Immediate Results*, 4th ed. Hoboken: John Wiley and Sons, Inc.

Bridges, William. 1991. *Managing Transitions: Making the Most of Change*. Cambridge, MA: Perseus Books.

Cannon, C. M. 2011. *An Executive's Guide to Fundraising Operations: Principles, Tools, and Trends*. Hoboken: John Wiley and Sons, Inc.

Carlone, K., and L. A. Hill. 2008. *Managing Up: Expert Solutions to Everyday Challenges*. Boston: Harvard Business School Press.

Clarke, M. 2005. *Leadership Land Mines: Eight Management Catastrophes and How to Avoid Them*. Chorley, UK: Scott Martin Productions.

"College Administrator Data/Turnover Rates: 2016–Present." 2018. *HigherEd™ Direct*, April 12, 2018. Higher Education Publications, Inc. https://hepinc.com/newsroom/college-administrator-data-turnover-rates-2016-present/.

Collins, J. C. 2001. *Good to Great: Why Some Companies Make the Leap and Others Don't*. New York: Harper Collins.

Covey, S. R. 1989. *The 7 Habits of Highly Effective People.* New York: Free Press.

Dobson, M. S., and D. S. Dobson. 2002. *Managing Up: 59 Ways to Build a Career-Advancing Relationship with Your Boss.* New York: Amacom.

Drucker, P. 2006. *The Effective Executive: The Definitive Guide to Getting the Right Things Done.* New York: Harper Business.

Gabarro, J. J., and J. P. Kotter. 2008. *Managing Your Boss,* Harvard Business Review Classics. Boston: Harvard Business School Press.

Gmelch, W. H., and J. L. Buller. 2015. *Building Academic Leadership Capacity: A Guide to Best Practices.* Hoboken: John Wiley and Sons, Inc.

Godin, K., and J. Hansen. 2015. "Physical task stress and speaker variability in voice quality." *EURASIP Journal on Audio Speech and Music Processing.* October 8, 2015. https://doi.org/10.1186/s13636-015-0072-7.

Goldstein, L. 2005. *College and University Budgeting.* Washington, D.C.: National Association of College and University Budget Officers.

Gunsalus, C., E. Luckman, N. Burbules, and S. Wraight. 2019. "Why Listening Matters for Leaders." *Inside Higher Education.* October 24, 2019. https://www.insidehighered.com/advice/2019/10/24/why-and-how-academic-leaders-should-become-better-listeners-opinion.

Harari, O. 2002. *The Leadership Secrets of Colin Powell.* New York: McGraw-Hill Professional Publishing.

Higher Education Directory. 2017. Reston, VA: Higher Education Publications, Inc.

"How is Interim Leadership Different than Traditional Leadership?" *Third Sector Company* (blog). April 19, 2017. https://thirdsectorcompany.com/interim-leadership-different-traditional-leadership/.

Hunt, P. C. 2012. *Development for Academic Leaders: A Practical Guide for Fundraising Success.* Hoboken: John Wiley and Sons, Inc.

Kotter, J. P. 1985. *Power and Influence: Beyond Formal Authority.* New York: Free Press.

Maxwell, John. 2011. "Leadership Landmines." *Success* (blog). June 3, 2011. https://www.success.com/john-maxwell-leadership-landmines/.

Mayhew, L. B. 1979. *Surviving the Eighties: Strategies and Procedures for Solving Fiscal and Budget Problems* (Jossey-Bass Series in Higher Education). Hoboken: Jossey-Bass/Wiley.

Neeley, T., and P. Leonardi. 2011. "Effective Managers Say the Same Thing Twice (or More)." *Harvard Business Review* 89, no. 5 (May 2011): 38–39. https://www.hbs.edu/faculty/Pages/item.aspx?num=40231.

Peters, T., and R. Waterman. 2006. *In Search of Excellence: Lessons from America's Best-Run Companies.* New York: Harper Business.

Pichon, H. W. 2018. "To Interim or Not to Interim." *LMI Blog Spot* (blog), American Association of Blacks in Higher Education, Leadership and Mentoring Institute. October 6, 2018. http://lmiexperience.org/to-interim-or-not-to-interim/.

Robbins, H., and M. Finley. 2003. *The Accidental Leader: What to Do When You're Suddenly in Charge.* Hoboken: Jossey-Bass/Wiley.

Schwartz, T., J. Gomes, and C. McCarthy. 2011. *Be Excellent at Anything: The Four Keys to Transforming the Way We Work and Live.* New York: Free Press.

Shellenbarger, S. 2016. "How Managers Get 'Interim' Out of Their Titles." *Wall Street Journal,* August 30, 2016. https://www.wsj.com/articles/how-managers-get-interim-out-of-their-titles-1472572415.

Simon, B. 2017. "Everything You Need to Know about Team Assessments." *Smartsheet. com,* July 28, 2017 (modified September 8, 2021). https://www.smartsheet.com/all-about-team-assessments.

"The Unconventional Value of an Interim Leader." *Point B,.* https://www.pointb.com/documents/The%20Unconventional%20Value%20of%20an%20Interim%20Leader.pdf.

Vaillancourt, A. M. 2018. "Are You Sure You Want That Interim Job?" *Chronicle of Higher Education,* May 14, 2018. https://www.chronicle.com/article/Are-You-Sure-You-Want-That/243408.

Watkins, M. D. 2013. *The First 90 Days: Proven Strategies for Getting Up to Speed Faster and Smarter,* Updated and Expanded ed. Boston: Harvard Business Review Press.

Wilcox, J. 2018. "A Study of Interim Leaderships in Nonprofits." *Philanthropy Journal,* September 10, 2018. https://pj.news.chass.ncsu.edu/2018/09/10/a-study-of-interim-leadership-in-nonprofits/.

Zaniello, J. 2019. "In the Interim: Why Temporary Leaders Should Not Be Placeholders." *Vetted Solutions,* July 1, 2019. http://www.vettedsolutions.com/Sources/The_Importance_of_Interim_Executive_Leadership.pdf.

Index

About the Author

Daniel J. Bernardo has nearly 30 years of higher education administrative experience at various levels across the university. Currently he is a senior advisor to the president at Washington State University (WSU). In mid-2015 Bernardo was named interim president of WSU following the untimely death of President Elson S. Floyd and served in that role for one year. From 2013 through 2015, and again from mid-2016 through 2019, he served as WSU provost and executive vice president in both permanent and interim positions.

Prior to becoming provost, Bernardo served for eight years as vice president for agriculture and extension and dean of the College of Agricultural, Human, and Natural Resource Sciences (CAHNRS). As dean, he led efforts to reinvigorate WSU's food and agricultural programs, including raising over $220 million in private contributions to fund endowed chairs, facility improvements, and programmatic activities.

Before moving to WSU, Bernardo was professor and department head of agricultural economics at Kansas State University from 1995 to 2005 and he was on the agricultural economics faculty at Oklahoma State University from 1985 to 1995.

Bernardo has a Ph.D. in agricultural economics from WSU and a B.S. in agricultural and managerial economics from the University of California, Davis.